EARN AT HOME MUM

Jody Allen was made redundant in 2009 while on maternity leave and pregnant with her second child, born 12 months after the first baby. She started her website, Stay at Home Mum, to share her money-saving experiences while her family lived on one wage and it has since become Australia's biggest mothers' network. Jody now connects with hundreds of thousands of women and has created a successful business. Jody lives in Gympie, Queensland, with her husband and two boys.

stayathomemum.com.au
@stayathomemum
@StayHomeMum
@SAHMum

Also by Jody Allen

Once a Month Cooking

Live Well on Less

The $50 Weekly Shop

The $50 Weekly Shop Weekday Dinners

EARN AT HOME MUM

How to **BOOST YOUR INCOME** or
START YOUR OWN BUSINESS
FROM HOME

JODY ALLEN

EBURY
PRESS

EBURY PRESS

UK | USA | Canada | Ireland | Australia
India | New Zealand | South Africa | China

Ebury Press is part of the Penguin Random House group of companies
whose addresses can be found at global.penguinrandomhouse.com.

Penguin
Random House
Australia

First published by Ebury Press, 2021

Cover design by James Rendall © Penguin Random House Australia Pty Ltd
Cover illustrations by Shutterstock
Typeset in Minion Pro by Midland Typesetters, Australia

Printed and bound in Australia by Griffin Press, part of Ovato, an accredited
ISO AS/NZS 14001 Environmental Management Systems printer

A catalogue record for this
book is available from the
National Library of Australia

ISBN 978 014378 777 8

penguin.com.au

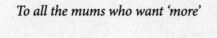

To all the mums who want 'more'

Table of Contents

Introduction

For me, working and earning at home is the best of both worlds. It means achieving a balance between making enough money to pay the bills, but still being around enough for my family. I love having the freedom to go to my children's rugby games or see them get an award at school. But I also love working online because I can set my own hours, I'm my own boss and I can work from home, which is my favourite place in the world. Plus I find the work challenging and engaging – certainly not boring!

As parents, we often feel that we are juggling more balls in the air than we can possibly handle. Long gone are the days when there was only one breadwinner whose wages were sufficient to support the whole family; now in most two-parent families, both parents have to work. And the cycle of rushing out to work, parenting, cooking, housekeeping and sleep, day in, day out, totally sucks.

This working and parenting pressure was unexpectedly increased in 2020 with the onset of the coronavirus pandemic. Many people had to juggle supporting their kids' remote learning alongside trying to do their job from home, usually with minimal preparation. However, this also gave many a taste of working from home and helped them to weigh up priorities, imagine lifestyle changes and explore new working possibilities for their post-pandemic life.

Even in 'normal' times, society expects a whole lot when it comes to the primary caregivers of children, which still tends to be women. There is an expectation that we pop out a few kids while we go to work full-time, keep on top of the housework, pay the bills, have time with our partner, take the kids to all their sports and activities, prepare meals for the family and still find time to exercise, have our nails done and our hair coiffed. The sheer pressure on us today is exhausting.

There are different reasons many of us want to earn extra income. Commonly cited reasons include:

- Independent income
- Family holiday
- Extra payments on the mortgage or credit card
- Pay down other debt
- Being able to afford little luxuries
- Fund extracurricular activities for your kids
- Build up your superannuation
- Freedom to go buy whatever you want

Whatever your reason, in the chapters that follow I'll show you ways to earn that extra cash, step by step. Just the same way I learned how to.

This book will not only teach you how to go about earning a living from your kitchen table, but also focus on business ideas aimed at mums that may well be something you could consider pursuing – because, let's face it, you rarely get rich working for other people.

So what does a mother-of-two from Gympie in rural Queensland know about earning from home? I've well and truly walked the path for the past decade, and it was something I was forced into out of necessity rather than something I started from a hobby or as a side hustle.

There's a quote by Hillary Clinton, which was attributed to Eleanor Roosevelt, that I've always felt drawn to: 'A woman is like a tea bag. You can't tell how strong she is until you put her in hot water.' Never has a quote felt as true for me as this one.

Ten years ago I found myself in hot water. I had two baby boys, my husband and I had started building our own home, and then I was made redundant from my secretarial job. We went from two good incomes down to one. We had the costs of a mortgage and renting at the same time, as well as the expenses that come with raising young children.

If we wanted to keep our new home, we had to maintain all our financial commitments on just a single income, which meant there was only $50 left to pay for food. And that's where Stay at Home Mum was born . . .

I started blogging about my struggles and asked mums on Facebook what they did to make ends meet. I quickly found there was a whole stack of other women out there in the same boat as me. It was a little piece of the internet made for mums to not only share their money-saving ideas, but to share how they used the internet to make a living for their families. Inspired by the challenges I was facing every day, this little money-saving blog had very humble beginnings, but it has grown into a full-blown parenting network read by millions of mums.

Don't for a second think I had a fairytale rags-to-riches storyline – I made every mistake in the book along the way! But I have detailed them all in *Earn At Home Mum* so you don't have to make them too.

I love that there is now a huge community sharing their ideas on the blog and website. These people, mostly women and mums, come to connect, to laugh about the stupid stuff that happens in life, and to vent frustrations about things only mums can fully comprehend.

If I can create something out of nothing and turn it into a successful business that is now paying my mortgage and putting way more than $50 worth of food on the table every week for my family, there's no reason why you can't take a passion of yours and find a way to make an income from it. This book is full of practical and sensible information, plus hundreds of ideas on what unique items or services to sell and where, how to market your products and ways to succeed on social media.

It's time to get fired up and start tapping into the resources you have access to from your home, and start earning great money doing something you love.

Now, let us begin!

Part 1

Research, prep and planning

Chapter 1

Why everyone should earn at home

It's official – earning at home is on trend! With a massive push from the COVID-19 global pandemic, so many people have been compelled to open their eyes to the benefits of working from home and just what is possible if you dare to think outside the rigid square of the nine-to-five rat-race.

It's not just mums wanting to earn extra cash on the side who are working at home now – many corporations and businesses have taken advantage of their employees working at home during the pandemic. Not only are their staff just as productive (if not more) while working from home, most of them are also happier without the stresses of the daily commute, saving both time and travelling expenses. Not only that, business owners are re-evaluating their need for the huge over-heads of office space and all the costs that go towards maintaining their premises. Working from home where possible has become a win–win situation. COVID-19 has forced the issue of cultural change for both workers and employers – and that aspect, at least, couldn't have come at a better time.

Online money-making opportunities are more available and access-ible than ever before. The global nature of the internet means you have access to millions of people who might be interested in the products or services you have to offer. Better still, because you are running the show, you get to decide what you create or market. You can do something that gets you excited and lights you up – and make money from it.

And on the other side, customers are accustomed to ordering goods and services online and having things delivered – we can shop from our bed while drinking a glass of wine!

Everyone *can* earn from home. And everyone can work around their busy family lives. The details are up to you.

1.1 The challenges and possibilities of working from home

At the time of writing, Australia is in the midst of the COVID-19 crisis. Millions of people worldwide have lost their jobs, and more and more people are looking at ways to become financially secure. Many are taking the power to earn an income into their own hands.

There is no better time to create a second or third source of income to protect yourself should you lose your current income or your circumstances change in other ways – to ensure that you can still put food on the table if the worst should happen. Independent income gives women not only financial security, but personal freedom as well. It doesn't take a global pandemic for your sense of job security to come under threat. It happened to me, and I really had to think on my feet so I could help provide for my family – the result is Stay At Home Mum!

My blog has become an online business that allows me to feed my children and to pay my mortgage. It has given me the freedom to work from home (which has always been my dream), together with my husband. It has opened so many doors I never would have dreamed possible, and it's led me to meet some incredible people along the way. Sure, it's been damn hard work, like any business. It took blood, sweat and tears to turn my idea into a reality.

You can create the same thing for yourself in whatever field of interest you have. All it takes is a lot of passion, consistency, determination and a desire to fulfil your dream. So many of us wax lyrical about the grand visions we have for the future – but do you have the gumption to make it a reality? I'm confident that you do.

If you look at the most successful businesspeople in the world, you'll notice that none of them rely on a single source of income. They all diversify. You too can do this – it'll just be on a smaller scale to start with. Remember: from little things, big things grow!

In the initial stages, you can focus on one or two aspects that will monetise your passion. Once you've established momentum and begin to earn, the trick is to keep an eye out for other opportunities that may come your way. This is how you can take the leap to diversify your offerings or start to collaborate with other businesses that have complementary products or services.

However, don't fall into the mindset trap that there is a magical business model you can use where you can 'set and forget' your business to work on total autopilot. This doesn't happen. All businesses need love and tweaking, especially when you are building from the ground up. You need to let people know that you exist and what you offer. Sure, there are businesses that aren't as hands-on as others, but they still need attention if they're to continue to grow and generate income.

If you are willing to put in the work, you can be successful.

1.2 The working-at-home rollercoaster

As with anything in life, there are benefits and pitfalls with working from home. I've experienced all of these at some stage or another since founding my business, so I know them well. Let's lay them all out so you can get a feel for whether this is the life for you.

Pros of working from home
You can do something you really love
No one willingly goes into a business because they *want* to work long hours for not much money at first while sacrificing time with their family. No – the reason we want to go into business is for money,

and to do something we love doing, *and* to be able to spend as much time with the family as we want to. When you've found that sweet spot that allows you to combine your passion with a way to earn a living, your whole life will change.

When you've been working nine-to-five for years on end, it can be hard to see the untapped potential of earning from home. You may even wonder how you can monetise your passion. Let me tell you: where there's a will, there's a way.

The beauty of the internet is that no two stories are ever the same. Many people have tried and failed, while others have tried and succeeded phenomenally. It's awesome when these people share their journeys, because it means others can learn what to do and what to avoid on their path to setting up a home business, or side hustle. Hell, there have been so many times I've tried something new and fallen on my face that I've lost count, but this is why finding your passion is so important. Without it, you won't get back up and try again.

If it inspires you, you will be motivated, determined and prepared to give it everything you've got. The best thing about doing something you really love is that you never feel like you're working. People are willing to pay you to do something you enjoy. Wouldn't you love a piece of that action?

Many of you already know which hobbies, products or services you are passionate about. But for those who are a little unsure, all it takes is a bit of reflection. Take some time to think back to conversations you've had in the past. There's always something that makes you smile from ear to ear whenever you talk about it. Something that, whenever someone asks about it, you can't stop talking about. Something that inspires every part of you.

When you find yourself reacting in this way, you know you're connected to it and that you'll feel fulfilled if you could make money from selling a product or service linked to it.

Now it's time to take that passion and run with it.

You can ensure financial independence
There are myriad horror stories out there about women who have supported their partners through further education, or who have stayed at home looking after the kids while their partner climbed the corporate ladder. Then one day the partner wants out or meets someone else – or perhaps even becomes ill or incapacitated through an accident. Where does that leave the woman?

Financially devastated.

Personal tip: Never ever EVER! totally rely on another person for all your financial needs.

This is a timely moment to also mention the gender pay gap, and how family responsibilities weigh heavier on women than men, affecting their career progression and contributing to systemic inequality. The full-time remuneration difference is a whopping 20.8% according to Workplace Gender Equality Agency data. In other words, men working full-time earn on average $25,679 a year more than women in the same role. And there has only been an improvement of 0.3% since November 2018.

Just to put the knife in and twist it that little bit more, women are far more likely than men to have little or no superannuation, due to years out of the workforce raising children. Women are twice as likely as men to have to sell their primary place of residence to move to a lower-cost accommodation because of tight financial circumstances. And women in their fifties and beyond are more likely to be homeless than any other age group.

Yes, the Motherhood Penalty isn't fair – but it's one of the strongest reasons to be the boss of your own domain.

You can set your work schedule

This means *you* decide if you want to stick to the traditional nine-to-five, Monday-to-Friday work week, or turn that completely on its head.

You might only want to work one day a week for seven hours, or three days a week for two hours. Or one week on, one week off might be appealing. Once you know how much time you'll need to commit each week to run your business effectively, you might choose to start the day earlier or later. You can take time to do the school run without stress, and then make up hours later that night or the next day if you need to.

Bye bye, travel time

With no workplace to travel to, you can kiss commuting goodbye! This means the money you would usually spend on fuel, public transport and parking can now go into your pocket. No travel to get to the office is one of my favourite aspects of working from home – I love not having to race anywhere to be at work. You will also find yourself with bonus time that you can invest wisely – finally, a chance to get some exercise in, or to build in some downtime to relax and recharge so you can operate on all cylinders all day long.

Working in pyjamas is a real thing

No corporate outfits to spend your hard-earned money on, no uniforms to prepare, no shirts to iron – what bliss! Working from home means you can embrace any style you like and, yes, trackies, pyjamas, active-wear and Ugg boots are definitely all valid (and comfortable) workwear choices. A hot tip, though: have one or two professional tops ready to pop on for any online meetings you may have with clients or business associates.

Flexible work space

Don't like the idea of one fixed workspace? Feel like a change of scene? No problem. Because you're at home, you can take your laptop outside, curl up on the couch or venture out to a cafe for an hour or two if you need some social interaction. The choice is all yours and you are free to do as you please.

It is nice to be in a quiet place and to be able to concentrate on an issue – no one visiting your desk to chat about anything or everything.

Cons of working from home
Blurred boundaries between home and business
With your place of work now in your home, it can be easy to slip into the habit of always being 'on'. Having defined times for work and family is very important. The pull towards the office to 'just check an email' can easily mean you break those boundaries. It's important to stay strong so you don't risk becoming a workaholic – it would be totally counter-productive to end up spending more time at work than you would if you were still employed in an office environment!

'Why can't you play, Mummy?'
Partners and children may take some time to get used to you working at home and not being available for interruptions every five minutes. You will need to educate your family about respecting the times you need to be left alone. However, interruptions can and will happen, and some-times you just have to go with the flow.

This is where you'll realise that flexibility is one of the benefits of being your own boss. If your family is having a restless day, don't fight the current – simply accept you won't be as productive that day, and then dive right in on the days when they're content to give you space.

The fridge is RIGHT THERE
This is my personal pitfall of working from home. The biscuits call my name like a siren. It's way too easy to get up and go to the kitchen. To overcome this, I've started packing my lunch daily when I do the kids' school lunches, and I try not to graze on other food. Hopefully you are more disciplined than me!

Risk of becoming sedentary

Having everything available at one desk is a blessing and a curse. You may find yourself spending too much time on your butt behind the computer instead of getting out regularly for fresh air. This comes down to discipline, and you just have to be extra-conscious about making your health a priority.

Because you're saving travel time every day, think of it as affording you time to exercise. Head out for a quick walk, or jump online and check out the huge array of free exercise routines you can do at home – anything from yoga to kickboxing is available, so choose whatever fits your mood and gets you pumped up for the day. If you're not a morning person, you can save your exercise break for the middle of the day or even the early afternoon to keep you focused.

Reduced social interaction

Working from home can be a dream for the introverts out there but a potential pitfall for the extroverts who love having people around them. If you find that you're missing social interaction, you can always make a point of catching up with a friend, client or potential client at least once a week. There are also plenty of co-working spaces you can pay to use, many of which you can use on a casual basis for those days when you have to get out of the house. Whenever you get the iso blues, just book a desk and head in for a couple of hours, or you can make it more regular if you are a fan of routine.

You could also join any one of a number of networking groups that are likely to be associated with your line of work. Head along to their events. Not only will this link you with like-minded people, but you can often learn some great new skills or gain insights into the minds of successful businesspeople in your area.

Distractions

Are you the type of person who has trouble focusing when you're at home rather than in a dedicated office environment? Some people have a magic ability to walk through the door of their home office and be 'on'. They are focused, they're in the zone and they can block out anything that's not directly related to their business during work time.

Others have what I call goldfish syndrome. Suddenly the washing urgently needs to be done, or the dishwasher beeps and must be emptied immediately, or the urge to click through to social media and begin the mindless scroll is just too great to ignore. If you suffer from this, you need to acknowledge it and put steps into place to help you focus.

I invested in a good pair of noise-cancelling headphones to put on while I work and now I listen to podcasts during my work hours, which blocks out all other distractions around me. But you can listen to silence, rainforest music or anything that will help you stay in the zone.

Conclusion

In this chapter, we've talked about working at home as a life balance choice – that you can earn an income and supervise your children at the same time. Sure, it still isn't easy, but at least you can be there. Another major upside is gaining financial independence, something for every woman to work towards; there's also the freedom of working on something that is your passion. And these are just the beginning of the many benefits for mums when it comes to earning money at home.

Chapter 2

You're just going to have to get over yourself

Women especially can be anxious when it comes to putting themselves out there. Yes, it is scary, but in order to grow, you have to suck it up and do things that make you uncomfortable sometimes.

Personally, I'm terrified of public speaking. I failed a subject at school because I refused to give my oral presentation in front of the class. I've taken lessons, hired private tutors, done everything to increase my public-speaking confidence – yet my legs still shake with fear.

But I still do it. I've been known to vomit before doing a television segment. More than once. I do it because it's good for my business, and because I want more and better for myself and for my family. Are you willing to go out on a limb and do something that terrifies you to help yours?

Perhaps you're still unsure about starting your earn-at-home journey, or you're lacking a feeling of confidence. Maybe you can think of any number of reasons why you shouldn't even take the risk because you tell yourself, 'Of course your enterprise is sure to fail.' The thing is, I've probably heard your doubts and reservations from loads of other people before – you're not alone – and I usually have an answer for them. Let's look at these now.

2.1 Common excuses and how to get past them

When it comes to doing anything new, it can be nerve-racking. But it's time to get over yourself and get out of your own way. Yes, there will be challenges. There'll be times when you wonder why the hell you're venturing off the well-beaten path. But at the end of the day, if what you are attempting was easy, everyone would be doing it!

Here are some of the excuses I've heard over the years from people wanting to go into small business, but who were unable to take the leap – and what you can do about it if these excuses have ever entered *your* mind.

'I don't have the time.'

Well, as the meme says, you have just as many hours in the day as Beyonce does – it's up to you how you manage that time. That said, parents are busy! You might have other responsibilities like caring for elderly parents or volunteering. But it all comes down to one thing: priorities. Can you get up earlier, work at night or dedicate half a day every weekend? The fact is, you will always *make* time for whatever is important enough to you.

Carry out a stocktake of how you spend your hours. You'll probably shock yourself with how many hours binging TV shows and social media scrolling can suck out of your day. This isn't about shaming, it's about awareness. Once you know what your time vampires are, you can banish them with garlic – or just schedule your day a little better in future.

If you start out well and then start to fall back into old habits, which can happen to the best of us, consider enlisting an accountability partner – someone you can check in with regularly to not only pep you up, but also to keep you on the straight and narrow.

'I'm afraid of failure.'

Failure to start is a guaranteed way to fail. As sporting legends such as Michael Jordan and hockey icon Wayne Gretzky have been reported to say, 'You miss 100% of the shots you don't take.'

Get over yourself – do what scares you and start! Even if you start a business, then fail, you have learned what not to do next time. Many of the world's greatest entrepreneurs openly say that without picking themselves up after every failure – the likes of Sir Richard Branson have had their fair share – they wouldn't have landed on the billion-dollar idea that catapulted them to success.

Remember that there is no shame in failure, especially if you can take those nuggets of learning to adjust your tack and move forward, but there *is* potential for a lot of regret if you let your dreams remain just that instead of taking action.

'I don't have enough money to start.'

Lack of money is not a good excuse to avoid getting the ball rolling. There are so many things you can do that don't require money. In fact, I think some of the best small businesses are those that have started on zero funds, because you are forced to get creative.

Aspects of your business that are free:

- Social media is free – and this is a great marketing tool for your product or service.
- Writing and sending press releases by email for your new business is free, and can net you coverage worth hundreds or even thousands of dollars.
- Talking to your customers via social channels is free. This builds trust in your brand and starts to build a community around your product or service.

If the small business you're wanting to launch really does need start-up funds, you can get cracking on looking into grant opportunities or seeking out investors to help you get a foothold. However, you don't have to place your future in the hands of others – work out what you can do in the meantime.

'There is too much competition out there.'

There will always be competition. But you can be better than they are. Go the extra mile. Make your product or service unique as only you know how.

Sometimes the point of difference is actually *you!* You could be selling exactly the same thing as someone else but people prefer to buy from someone they like. If you can bring your personality to the table, this might be the only thing you need to set you apart from the crowd.

If you can home in on a particular niche and connect specifically to them, you can outplay your competitors by becoming the go-to person for that section of the market. Have fun with it. You might be surprised at what you can come up with.

One more point to help settle this fear: women in particular are susceptible to subconsciously believing the myth of scarcity. By this I mean they think that if one person is doing well, there isn't room for you to do well too, in any field. But there *isn't* some finite amount of success to be used up, for which we're all in direct competition. There's room for everyone at this table, which includes you if you can find your passion and turn it into your niche business.

'I don't have the smarts.'

You don't need to have a business degree or even to have finished high school to start a successful business. All you need to get you rolling is passion and a desire to learn the basics. And no, that doesn't necessarily mean you have to enrol in formal education.

In fact, the more uniquely your mind works, the greater your ability to think beyond the box. This will give you an advantage over the majority of the players in business. People who follow a set formula taught in business education can find success, sure, but those who create their own formulas and rely on instinct and skills they learn along the way are often called 'disruptors', and become the new trendsetters in business. I know which one I'd rather be . . .

'I don't have the skills.'

Then learn the skills you need, or throw yourself in the deep end and learn as you go. It is amazing what you can learn on YouTube or by doing one of the thousands of free online courses out there. If you do want to get a more in-depth look at the skills you need to get started, you might consider applying for a scholarship to learn more. See if there are any people already operating with whom you can team up to learn together and bounce your ideas off.

Swap the hours of watching streaming services for reading business books; there are a gazillion out there that can help you to overcome your personal blocks and give you industry-specific tips, guidelines and processes on which you can model your early start-up.

There are also heaps of webinars online that you can attend, run by people who are experts in their field. Many of these are free and they share some great pearls of wisdom. Be aware, though, that a lot of these sessions will be backed up by a sales pitch of some kind; this is their way of marketing their business and converting interested people into clients (a tactic you may wish to employ as you grow your business, if it's service-based). Remember that you're not obligated to sign up for anything. You are well within your rights to watch the free content and move on.

'I don't know how to start.'

Two words: analysis paralysis. So many people get stuck in the 'how', and when they can't answer it, they abandon ship. Throwing yourself in the deep end and learning 'how' as you go is great too. It actually prevents you from suffering from analysis paralysis, because you can take it one step at a time. Once you find out what the first step is and complete it, the second step usually becomes clear.

If you look at how you're going to get from concept to six-figure business, for example, it can seem too overwhelming. The 'how' of getting from zero to that level can feel like a crapload of work, which really sucks all the fun out of it! So start small, one step at a time. When a 'how' question appears, talk to people already in business or seek out the answers as you need them, by googling, using YouTube or asking people you know who've done it before. You will save many wasted hours learning skills you may never need or paying for courses that won't actually help you to achieve your goal, all because you felt you had to know everything before proceeding.

'Everyone says it won't work out.'

Lack of support from partners, family or friends is a really common issue. In fact, sometimes it's the people we value and trust the most who can be our biggest handbrakes. It can hurt when you're brimming with excitement about your new venture, only to be told by someone close to you that it's a pipe dream and that you will never be able to pull it off.

This can be a sign of jealousy. They don't want you to succeed because then you might do better than them. It could also be fear on their part that you'll change or move on from them when you find success. They'll be left in the dust if they can't keep up with you. Remember, these are *their* issues to deal with. Don't let them stop you from giving it a go. In fact, make the naysayers an incentive to do better!

Look, I adore my parents, but they don't really understand exactly what I do – so sometimes they tell me to go get a real job! Rather than let this become a bugbear in our relationship, I just accept that they don't really understand the nature of the internet – and that they just want me to have secure employment.

Think about all the people in your life who have given new things a go and do your best to support them, whether in person or just leaving them a positive message on social media. Put it out to the universe that you'll support others, and that will come back to you.

I'm so lucky to have support all around me. To show what a support-ive partner can mean to your sense of confidence, I've asked my husband, Brendan, to give his point of view.

A partner's point of view – Brendan Allen

Hello there. My beautiful wife Jody has asked me for my thoughts on what it's like to support someone who wants to start earning money from home. To be honest, I'm super glad for the chance to contribute to her book. Supporting her is kind of my thing.

So, where to start? Hey, let's start at the start.

You have an amazing idea and you're starting to get your ducks in a row. Okay, great, but I'm going to stop you right there. We need to tick a box. Did you get the blessing and support of your partner for this venture?

Yeah, I know – how deflating! But no, I am not asking did you get their consent – that's a completely different thing. To allow this seed of an idea to take root, you need to have their unwavering support. Starting a business from scratch is really hard, and if your partner isn't going to support you, it will tear a rift in your relationship that will be nigh on impossible to mend.

Take Jody's and my story, for example. I come from a self-employed family that has always been entrepreneurial. Early on in our relationship, Jody and I realised that we were on a runaway train to self-employment. We didn't know how, what or when, but we knew it was in our future.

We looked high and low for a business to buy or an idea for something to start. Jody was a full-time stay-at-home mum to our two boys and I was working for a boss, selling my life (and soul) by the hour. Lo and behold, the opportunity of Stay at Home Mum came along, and we picked it up and ran with it for all our worth.

I was still working 60 hours a week and Jody was doing between 80 and 100 hours a week in the early days. It became clear that with two young boys to raise, this whole endeavour was going to end in tears and broken dreams without proper management and support.

As Jody's husband and partner, I was already her biggest fan, but I realised this was my time to step up my game. Without any need for a formal discussion, we fell into a natural lead-and-support arrangement. I became the earthmover who tried my best to clear a path for Jody. This wasn't the way we thought things would go, but I loved it. In the early days, bootstrapping along and taking every opportunity to further the business together formed memories that we will treasure forever.

So, put this book down, walk over to your partner and say, 'You better support me in this, 'cause one day I'll be employing you.' Then laugh together, and tell them to make you a cup of tea.

2.2 Why mums make such good entrepreneurs

Having put paid to many of the common fears that hold women back from plucking up the courage to start their own business, there's a further reason to see yourself as capable, strong and suited to any challenge chasing your dreams might hold: mums make the perfect entrepreneurs.

Think about it. We're well-versed in being organised, we can multi-task, we've got loads of experience in dealing with problems by thinking on our feet, we know *all* about hard work, and we're accustomed to sacrifice and delayed gratification. These are all perfect traits for the budding entrepreneur.

Think about all the skills you've acquired in your parenting, and consider how you can draw on them in setting up a new business. You'll be a natural.

Conclusion

It's daunting for any busy mum to pursue new endeavours and passions – the dream of turning them into money-making ventures is sure to bring out doubts and second guessing – but there are so many reasons not to give up.

I hope this chapter has answered at least some of your doubts – and that you're feeling strong and confident about all the possibilities your future holds. Next step, plan for your success.

Chapter 3
Setting yourself up for success

Now you've overcome your mental barriers and moved through the common excuses to a place where you're feeling pumped and ready to become an at-home money generator, it's time to start some research and planning.

In this chapter, you'll get out the notebook and have a good, honest look at what you want from your new working life, how you'll achieve it and what passions you can draw from to keep you inspired. You'll think about the practicalities and make some plans. And of course it's always great to have some tricks up your sleeve to help you get past any challenges that may come your way, so I'll focus on those too!

3.1 Your financial non-negotiables

You have bills to pay, so there isn't any point of spending all your energy setting something up that doesn't meet your financial needs. It's time to sit down and work out all the aspects of your new earning strategy that are non-negotiable. This information will then help you choose the right online path to take. So, grab a piece of paper and write down your answers to these questions.

Questions to ask	Details to think about
What is the minimum weekly/ monthly amount of money I require?	Take into account your partner's income (if you have a partner), rent or mortgage, utility bills, food, insurance, childcare – any fixed costs.
How many hours per week is doable to balance family and work?	Can you reasonably do two hours per day, or ten hours per day? Do you have access to childcare?
What areas am I passionate about?	If you're going to be spending lots of time at work, you need to like what you do. What do you like to do? Do you like to work outside, or on the computer? Are you interested in history, or do you love cars? Whatever your preferences and tastes, note them down here.
What am I good at?	You know what you are good at – put that here too!
Where do you see yourself in one year, five years and ten years?	Do you want to own your home, be the CEO of a company, be debt-free or just have more time to spend at home with the family?

Once you've answered all these questions, you have your non-negotiables and can go into a business or side hustle knowing exactly what characteristics that that job must have.

3.2 Work–home balance

Juggling a full-time job, kids, the house, a partner and extended family seems exhausting at the best of times. I'm not going to sugarcoat it – when starting a new business all of that only gets harder. You have to be willing to put in the work, especially when getting it off the ground. And this means cutting into 'fun' time.

I like to think that investing this time is like putting money in the bank for a rainy day – sure, it isn't fun now, but it is buying you security and perhaps even regaining 'fun' time in the long term.

So how do you manage it all?

Always put your immediate family first. If you have little children, they are only little once. Work around their sleep schedule. Get up early so you have time in the morning while it's quiet, or use the evening hours after you've put them to bed. Be as organised as you can in running your family life so that it allows more time for you to work on your business.

As mentioned in the previous chapter, having a partner who will support you in your business endeavours will help enormously – they'll need to help out in areas they might not usually in order to help you carve out those hours to get your work done.

Here are some of my keys to managing life and business:

- Have a family calendar – put all the important kid-related dates in there first.
- Put aside time for both family and business every single day. The key to success in both is consistency. Keep family time as family time and business time for business as much as you can.
- Invest in noise-cancelling headphones for when you're working on your business – they really help with focus.
- Plan your days in advance for maximum efficiency. What are your top three things you want to get done? Prioritise those first, and then see what else you have time for. Some days you might only get one thing done, but that's okay.

- Use a project management tool to ensure that you get everything you need to do for your business done properly and on time. There are loads of great apps out there that will ensure you never miss a single thing. Basecamp, Trello and Asana are some popular ones.
- Become a planner. Planning is everything when you're working for yourself. Do your research about your product. Plan it well. Go ahead! But most importantly, stick to your plan. There might be challenges along the way that mean you need to tweak a bit, but don't ever give up.
- Make use of available services. Many small business owners work at night when their kids are asleep. It's actually an ideal time to go about your business since you won't be bothered by your kids, although your own lack of sleep may stress you out and isn't healthy long term. So it's important to take a rest when you can, but avoid taking this approach every night. Other mumpreneurs prefer dropping their kids off at daycare and spending a few solid hours working on their business.
- For mums who find it hard to concentrate at home with all the distractions, try a co-working space in your area. Seeing like-minded entrepreneurs working can motivate you as well. Some co-working spaces also have childcare services, a brilliant way to get around juggling your business and kids at the same time at home.

3.3 Set up a workspace

There is romance around the idea that now you're free from the office grind, you can become a satellite entrepreneur who travels the world working from the laptop – heck, if that's your dream, then go for it!

But even the most well-travelled entrepreneur has a home base that they can return to, and creating a workspace at home is a must. For those who haven't had to do this before, here are the basics.

Find a place for your home office

If you have an office or a spare room at home, you're winning already. If you don't, you'll need to create a space where you can set up a laptop or desktop computer without being in the way of anything or anyone.

One common concern about setting up a home office is the lack of space if you have a small house or apartment. Using the living room or your bedroom may not be ideal, but it'll work in the short term. Don't let a lack of space stop you from getting started.

Setting up your laptop on a kitchen bench works well as a low-cost stand-up desk – just adjust the height with some books to make it more ergonomic so you're not hunching over for hours. If you have a little bit of cash to spend on setting up an office, you can invest in a proper stand-up desk that you can set on the dining table, or a platform that you can pop over your lap to rest your laptop on for added height. A separate keyboard and mouse will be useful too.

A laptop tray desk will allow you to work from a bed or anywhere. Add your phone, and now your mobile home office is ready for work. You can take your tray, computer and phone anywhere! I have a lap desk I found at a secondhand store, and it's fabulous for when I want to take my work outside or to an armchair in the living room.

What do you really need?
Here's a quick list of the essentials to get you started. But offices aren't just about practicality – you also need a space that inspires you. This might mean you put up posters or pictures to personalise your space, for example, along with the following basics:

- A dedicated desk, ideally, or portable lap tray
- Laptop/desktop computer
- Mobile phone
- Internet connection – NBN or broadband would be ideal, or you can use your phone as a hotspot
- Stationery – notepads, pens, pencils, diary or planner if needed

Great apps for working at home
For working on your phone or computer, you may want to check out some of the following apps.

Team communication apps:

- Slack
- Skype
- Zoom

Time management apps:

- Trello
- Basecamp
- Asana

Newsletter apps:

- Mailchimp

Storage apps:

- Dropbox

Word processing apps:

- G Suite

Networking apps:

- LinkedIn

Payment apps:

- PayPal
- Stripe
- Square

Finance and accounting apps:

- Xero
- QuickBooks
- Wave

Social media scheduling apps:

- Buffer
- Hootsuite

Have a vision board

It might sound laughably over the top, but creating a vision board, or even just a list, can really motivate you to achieve your goals or at least help you work harder towards them. It doesn't have to be anything fancy – just a collection of images you find inspiring or a list of the things you want in life. Stick them on a piece of paper or write them down and put the list somewhere you can see them every single day – pin it up on the wall in your workspace, or stick it on your fridge. You can use a Pinterest board for this too, but I prefer to keep something physical where I see it every day to really keep my goals at the forefront of my mind.

The goals on my first vision board took five years to complete. I'm on my second one now and keeping that list front and centre makes me strive to achieve it all.

What to do if you have kids at home?

If your partner can look after the kids while you're working, that's the ideal situation if they're available and willing to do so. If your partner needs to work as well, you might need to get creative around how you spend your time. Perhaps you can spend the day with the kids, and when your partner finishes their work, they move into carer duty so you can work.

For single parents, first of all, my hat goes off to you – you are amazing. Finding a good activity to keep the kids occupied is the key. Let the kids exhaust themselves in the backyard or on the swings at the local playground while you station yourself on a bench with your laptop; if the weather isn't kind, put on a movie to keep them quiet for the time you need to concentrate the most.

When my kids were little I used to get up early (*really* early) and work for an hour or two before they woke up. It was a beautiful, quiet time of day with no interruptions, I got a lot of shit done. You might also be able to grab a few hours here and there with help from a relative, friend or neighbour – maybe you can take turns having a friend's kids for an afternoon while they work on their own projects or have some me-time, and then they take yours so you can work on your business.

If you're stuck in the work–mum juggle, here are some activities you can give kids to do while you're working:

- Make figures with playdough.
- Draw or colour.
- Watch a favourite show.

- Play an educational game on the iPad.
- Read a book if they can, or look through a picture book if they're younger.
- Play with board games or packs of cards (I taught my boys how to play solitaire and it kept them occupied for hours).
- Do a jigsaw.
- Download a kids' book on Audible and play it to them.

Hot tip: If your kids are drawing or playing with playdough, it's wise to check regularly that they're not decorating the living room or furniture with their artwork! This has happened to me before – crayon all over the couch covers…

Don't worry if the kids are hard work one day and you just can't get things done – it happens. Remember, there is always tomorrow!

3.4 My tips for a productive work day

Start the day right

Taking some time to relax and focus before you start the day is a good idea. This can look different for each person. I like to slug down a few coffees in bed and read the news on my phone before even thinking about starting the day. But do what works for you: go for a walk, do an exercise class or watch some trashy television – anything that clears your mind.

Whatever helps you to relax is a goer. My routine sets me up to be more focused and able to react to any issues that crop up. It only needs to be a few minutes.

Put on your daily uniform

When you talk about working from home, people automatically think that you wear your pyjamas all day – and if you want to, you can! However, if you have trouble getting into the flow or habit of sitting down to work, it really can help to get up in the morning and dress for work.

This doesn't mean you need to put on a suit. I wear activewear every day – that's my uniform. I know that as soon as I'm dressed for work, I'm ready to actually work – plus I don't have to change when I exercise later in the day, so less washing! #winning

Find your own version of a daily uniform and your brain will soon associate that uniform with work.

Routine is queen

If you're working from home and have kids to get off to daycare or school, routine is the key. Not only is it good for you, it's good for the family. Everyone knows what's expected of them every morning.

I freeze lunches for my kids in batches so that I can quickly throw together their lunchboxes in the mornings. The kids have a checklist to follow: showers, DEODORANT, put on uniform, breakfast, brush teeth, pack your bags and out on time, ready or not.

Cut the distractions

With the kids out of the house, it's time to remove distractions on your computer and phone. Close browser windows and turn off app notifications to allow you to concentrate on your work. You can use a productivity app like Forest to help you to stay focused. Tell family and friends that you're busy at certain times, which can help you to set up expectations about your time and availability.

Take regular breaks

When you work for an employer, they're legally required to ensure you have sufficient breaks throughout the day so you aren't overworked. Now that you are your own boss, you need to make sure you honour this for yourself. When you work from home, you don't have anyone telling you to stop or even when you should have lunch – your time is up to you. Make sure to stop every hour to give your eyes a rest and to look at something else – too much screen time will hurt your eyes, so head outside and focus on some distant trees/nature.

When you have a break, don't just switch over to social media – get up and walk around, do a few simple stretches and make sure to be away from your desk and phone for a little bit.

Sustenance

Set a time where you down tools to make yourself some lunch and take a break. For example, you could have a dedicated lunch hour from twelve until one. It can be easy to get carried away in your work and suddenly it's time to pick the kids up from school, and you haven't had anything to eat since before you dropped them off in the morning! Make a sandwich and eat it outside, or put on your favourite show or podcast and relax for a while.

If you're missing the fancy café lunches, perhaps you can head out once a week to meet with like-minded friends and treat yourselves. This will break up the monotony of foraging in the pantry and fridge.

Connect

Make time to network and meet others in similar fields. Join your local Chamber of Commerce and follow local business Facebook pages. These people will help you with ideas, problems or issues, and can also refer their family and friends to your business. Plus many of these groups are the first to be aware of any funding or grant opportunities that you may be able to take advantage of.

Dress for the occasion

If you have a video conference with your team or a client, make sure to dress nicely. If you really begrudge having to take off your pyjamas or trackies, at least make sure your top half is respectable. Newsreaders do it; so can you.

Be careful of your backdrop

Be mindful of your backdrop for video conference meetings. Do a quick check of the scene behind you before you open the meeting to your guests, and get rid of dirty clothes, piles of toys and other things that tend to collect in the background.

Remember, you don't want other people to see any sensitive business information up on a whiteboard behind you in a meeting. If possible, have your back to a wall or set of curtains. Look up more tips on video conferencing on YouTube – it is a wealth of information.

3.5 Learn to upskill

Having a business, no matter how big or small, will teach you skills that will come in handy for every aspect of your life.

They say the first step is always the hardest, and making the commitment to give it a go is the very first step to take – so well done if that's where you are! Perhaps the next step in preparing to run your own show is to honestly assess what skills you'll need to be efficient, competitive and ultimately successful. Upskilling is empowering, can be fun and interesting, and will protect you and your business for the future.

If you've been out of the workforce for a few years while raising your family, consider whether you need a refresher in your chosen area – for example, think of how quickly technology moves on. There may be aspects of running a business that are completely new to you and you need to learn from scratch.

You don't have to have a business degree, or even to have paid attention to economics in high school to find great success in your own business. There are many industries where you get the most experience from learning on the job, and creating a new business is no exception. If you think your business skills are lacking, though, or if you feel you don't even know what you don't know, it's never too late to start learning! There are so many places online now where you can learn those skills, often for free.

Beginning to upskill can be as basic as watching YouTube tutorials (just about everything is on YouTube these days) through to short courses or TAFE, or even a university degree if you're prepared to really launch into it. Find something that fits your time and budget.

You can't go wrong by visiting your local library and taking out some business books to both learn from and find inspiration. Some of my recommendations include:

- *The Personal MBA* by Josh Kaufman
- *Thrive* by Arianna Huffington
- *So Good They Can't Ignore You* by Cal Newport
- *The Subtle Art of Not Giving a F*ck* by Mark Manson
- *Get Over Your Damn Self* by Romi Neustadt
- *The 80/20 Principle* by Richard Koch
- *The Freaks Shall Inherit the Earth* by Chris Brogan

3.6 You never know who is watching

Remember all those old stories about talent scouts hiding away in pubs and clubs waiting to find the next big thing to take the music industry by storm, swooping the unsuspecting performers into contracts that catapulted them to international fame and fortune? Okay, that's an extreme example, but the fact is, you never know who's watching what you're doing and what you're achieving and how it can affect your plans or even your fledgling business.

Stepping up and putting yourself out there can have amazing and completely unexpected benefits. Here you are, just doing your thing and loving life while making money – and all of a sudden, you get a phone call with an offer of a book contract from a publisher who has seen you create an amazing following behind your brand. Or maybe it's an email with a request for an interview on a national television show that will showcase you and your business to the whole country . . .

My story of being 'discovered'

In about year two of Stay at Home Mum, I had a phone call from an older gentleman who wanted to invest money into my business. I thought, 'Who rings a random and offers them money – dodgy AF!' I thanked him (well, I think I actually said, 'Yeah, right!'), hung up and put the whole thing from my mind.

Three days later I got a call from the man's daughter, who happened to be one of my advertisers, to tell me that her dad was the real deal. This led to a very successful partnership – and to this day he laughs about that initial phone call.

The key to this is getting yourself in front of as many people as possible to increase the chance of this happening, and this lies squarely in how you market yourself and your business. We'll be covering this in detail in Chapter 9.

3.7 Learn from someone with experience

Working from home means you don't have the benefit of being able to ask a colleague or supervisor questions about how to proceed if you ever find yourself stuck. When you're starting out working from home or still in the planning stage, having someone you can call on for feedback or advice is priceless.

Picking the brains of someone who is already in the business but not a competitor is a fantastic way to learn. They have already walked the path you're on; perhaps they've fallen on their face a few times and have that experience they can share with you. In this way, you can avoid the common pitfalls of starting a new business, both in general terms and in matters specific to your shared area.

Perhaps it's someone you used to work with or who was connected to your old workplace in some way, and you can reach out to them. As another option, many Facebook groups now have a Mentorship option, where people are offering to be mentors to others – take people up on this and don't be scared to ask all the hard questions.

Of course, not everyone is suited to having a mentor. Some people need to find their own way – often the hard way. If that's you, that's okay too.

Conclusion

There's so much to consider when contemplating a big life change like forming your own business, and in this chapter we dug deep into the planning. You need to decide how to set yourself up, where you'll work, what to do with the kids when you need a productive day, who you can ask for advice, whether you should upskill . . . The list might seem insurmountable, but sitting down with paper and pen and and taking an honest look at how you can get this show on the road will get you much of the way there.

In the next part of this book, you can put all this thinking and planning to use in deciding what form your earning-at-home life will take, whether it be making money on the side, making a career from a hobby, or launching an online business based on a passion. Let's go!

Part 2

Casual ways to earn

Chapter 4
Casual earning online

Having looked at all the ways that setting up your own business can work wonders for you, your finances and your lifestyle, perhaps you feel like dipping a toe in the water first, rather than taking a big leap. You might have been out of the workforce on maternity leave and are just now starting to think about what your working future could look like once you start getting some decent sleep, or you might need to generate some income sooner than starting up your own business would allow.

A good place to start if you're not ready to start a fully-fledged business is with some casual earning online. You may not need to go through all the hassle of setting up a business name, ABN and so on (though you do need to keep records of your earnings for tax purposes), but you can start learning skills that you can turn into a more profitable business down the track.

4.1 Ways to dip your toe in

Let's look at a range of ways to make money online before you launch into starting your own business. Perhaps you could try a few to see what fits, and what experience you might be able to apply to starting your own business in time to come. Because these are online earning methods, you'll find there is a lot of information available online to help you get started and get the most out of it.

Complete online surveys

One super low commitment way of entering the world of online earning is to do online surveys for payment or gift cards. Doing these on a regular basis will make you money, just not a lot of it – perhaps a few hundred dollars per year, if that. Many people enjoy participating in surveys and thinking about what might attract them to a product or service, so the small return is a nice bonus for your time. It might be worthwhile as something you can fit around all the other tasks in your busy life, exactly when it suits you, so let's look at what it involves.

The biggest problem with most survey sites is that they are often looking for participants from specific demographics – and they pay well if you meet their strict criteria. However, if you're not in that demographic, they might not need you at all or will only pay low rates.

Always check one of the many online survey review sites before signing up to do a survey. People are brutally honest about their experiences with them – and then you know the pitfalls and whether it is even worth joining that particular platform. The largest complaint I have seen about many survey sites is that many are notorious for cancelling your membership when you go to cash out your rewards – or they won't respond to any emails questioning this. If a site is not legitimate, they may sell your email address and information to other companies, which means you'll be inundated with spammy emails. Go into online surveys with your eyes open – and a dedicated email address you've set up just for this purpose!

Here are some of the best-known sites where you can look for surveys to participate in.

Survey Junkie Australia is one of the oldest and more well-known paid online survey sites. It rewards you in points for each survey that you complete. One hundred points is equal to $1 in value – and once your threshold reaches $10, you can cash out in money or gift cards. It's free to sign up, you get bonus points for tasks you can do when signing up, and it is easy to use. One negative is that it has a limited survey offering.

Valued Opinions Australia is an Australian-based paid online survey site that has a lot of very interesting and different kinds of surveys available to do. However, there are a limited supply of surveys to actually do. It seems that, like most survey sites, you need to qualify in order to get the highest-paying surveys. Payment is via gift cards for a number of well-known brands.

Swagbucks is one of the larger online survey sites, with over 20 million registered users worldwide. You can earn points for various actions such as taking surveys, playing games, shopping online using their discount codes, and watching advertising videos. All these actions award you points that are then redeemed for either cash or gift cards. Swagbucks seems to have a lot more offerings survey-wise than other survey sites; however, many of these paid online surveys are provided by third parties, which means you can find yourself signing up a few times instead of just the once.

LiveTribe is another online survey site that's based in Australia. It offers online surveys, competitions and gaming tasks, and also a $5000 sweepstakes giveaway you can enter by participating in any of the actions on the site. You get additional points for completing your profile and following their social media channels. Rewards include either cash or e-vouchers.

Pureprofile is a Sydney-based survey website that offers cash, movie vouchers and retail vouchers in exchange for doing surveys that you must qualify for first. Pureprofile has a minimum cash-out of $25 that's paid via PayPal. The great thing about Pureprofile is that if you refer friends and family to the website, you can earn $2 for each person referred, as long as they complete two campaigns within 30 days of becoming a member. When you sign up to the site, it will take you through multiple questions to determine what campaigns will be a good fit for you.

Write product reviews

Try out a product and write a review about it. Like doing surveys, you're not going to cover your mortgage by writing product reviews, but it's a good way to start small. Many brands are keen to know what consumers think, so that feedback will help them improve their product. While some companies send free products for you to review, others just offer a discount when you buy one. Some companies also offer incentives.

An especially good place to find product reviewing requests is on parenting websites – I've seen pram companies pay $100 per review.

Evaluate websites

Bloggers and website owners want to make sure their website is working properly for users, so some pay for objective reviews from a number of people. To evaluate websites, you'll need to be objective and internet savvy, since you'll need a basic understanding on how it works.

Here are some examples of where to get work evaluating websites:

- UserTesting
- Respondent
- TestingTime
- TryMyUI
- Userfeel
- Userbrain
- Userlytics
- UTest

Moderate Facebook groups

If you have a Facebook account and are a part of any Facebook group, you'll know how out of hand some participants can get! That's why many large groups employ Facebook moderators to watch their social media pages and ensure that the members are adhering to the rules of the group.

This isn't a huge paying job and there mightn't be many hours in it, but you can expect up to $20 per hour or a couple of free products every year in return. Keep in mind that you'll need to check in frequently.

Use your language skills as a translator or interpreter

There is always a demand for translating and interpreting skills, and while many careers use this skill, there are ways to earn casually online as well. If you can speak more than one language, you might be able to earn some money completing transcriptions or small freelance translating jobs. Have a look at:

- The Translating and Interpreting Service (Australia)
- Upwork
- Gengo
- Smartling

How much you can expect to make really depends on the language you speak and how many other translators there are, how well you can speak it, and whether you can write the language as well as speak it, but you can expect a base of at least $30 per hour.

Data entry work

There are a lot of data entry jobs out there, and it's one of the most convenient options for SAHMs as most let you set the number of hours you can fit in each week around your family commitments. Data entry jobs vary from one company to another but basically, it involves inputting different types of data into a program or spreadsheet for a company. You will need extreme focus and attention to detail. You also need to be reliable and organised, as you're in charge of making sure all information is accurate.

Provide transcription services

If you can type quickly and accurately, why not be a freelance transcriptionist? Work can be found in the medical or legal spheres as well as many other industries. This involves listening to a recording and typing out the content word for word. You need a computer and excellent internet connection. You should be detail-oriented, organised and have the ability to type at a competitive level of words per minute. Medical transcriptionists can expect to be paid from $50 to $80 per hour and rates vary in other areas.

Become a podcaster

If you have a smartphone and a good microphone, why not look at starting a podcast? You name the topic – there is a podcast on it. With a bit of producing work to ensure that the intros and outros are seamless, and a bit of licensed music, you're good to go.

There isn't any payment for doing podcasts until you get enough followers to be able to charge advertising dollars – but if your podcast takes off, really big dollars can be made.

Trending topic ideas include:

- True crime
- Sex and relationships
- Business
- Science
- History

Buy and sell items

Many people who want to earn money from home try this method first. If you need extra cash right away, selling what's right in front of you is often the easiest way to get it.

This is a great way to get rid of clutter, such as unwanted gifts or outgrown toys, but it isn't a long-term moneymaking solution. You need dedicated products, aimed at a dedicated audience, to sustain your income. To buy and sell items as an ongoing business in this casual context, you need to stick with what you know, and what you know isn't necessarily what you like.

The problem most of us have is that we know the market well, but we don't have a niche product. For example, many mums choose to sell fashion – it's something they're interested in and have on hand to sell. The problem with fashion is that it's a saturated market with not a lot of mark-up value. You would need to sell a whole lot of fashion on a regular basis to bring in enough money to make a living.

The most successful items to sell on platforms like eBay include:

- Vehicles
- University textbooks
- Sporting equipment
- Musical instruments
- Vintage electronics
- Vintage toys
- High-end brand shoes

The reason they make money is that usually the purchaser (that is, you before you re-sell) can upgrade or fix the item, or the items might be rare and there is a big demand for them.

When you want success in a field, you look to who is already doing well at it – what are their tricks? Check out the successful eBay or Etsy sellers. What do you notice about what they're doing?

This is what I have observed:

- Their images are clear, large and engaging, and there are plenty of them.
- They provide excellent customer service; therefore, their feedback scores are high.
- Their item descriptions are very detailed and spell-checked, and address all the frequently asked questions.
- They respond quickly to queries from customers.

Hot tip: Look for items that are listed in the wrong section, or contain a major spelling mistake, as others are likely to overlook these, meaning you'll snap up a great deal! A good example is the shoe brand Skechers. If you look on Ebay for 'Sketchers' (notice it is spelled incorrectly, an easy mistake to make), there are loads of listings there. Yes, using other people's mistakes to make money seems somewhat sordid – but the game is the game.

Get jobs from small job apps

If you don't have time to start a small business, taking on a variety of tasks via small job apps or sites is a quick way to make a buck. The main app for this is Airtasker, which lets people outsource small jobs around the home to others. People post a description of the job that needs to be done, where the job is, what the requirements are, and propose a fair budget. Then you can apply to do the work – and if the poster chooses you, you go ahead and do the task and receive the payment in your bank account within a day or two. There are all sorts of jobs on Airtasker, from house cleaning to plumbing, rubbish removal to delivery services, clothing alterations to dog-walking.

Check out what other people want done or are offering to do for others. Think about what skills you have and what equipment you can utilise that could allow you to do small jobs. For example, I hate organising photos and I would happily employ someone else to do it for me! Imagine: these days we all have literally thousands of photographs on multiple devices all around the home, photographs that need to be sorted, perhaps printed and placed in albums in some sort of order. This is a time-consuming job but if you love organising and have a good attention to detail, it could be a perfect job opportunity.

Rent out your stuff

I know I said that you can't make a sustainable income from selling your own items, but take a look at all the stuff you have around your home – and your home itself. You could be sitting on a goldmine without even realising it – if you rent instead of sell.

Rent out your wardrobe

Do you have a passion for fashion and a closet that is bursting at the seams as a result? Don't let those amazing outfits hang there gathering dust – rent them out! Everything from shoes and accessories to clothing and jewellery is in demand for school formals, weddings, corporate events and black tie awards evenings.

Platforms where you can rent out your clothing include:

- The Volte
- Glam Corner (Sydney-based)
- Designerex

Rent out your backyard

If you live in an area with wide open spaces, there is an app called Hipcamp Australia that allows you to hire out your garden to people who want to get out of the city and pitch their tent somewhere secure – such as your property. If you have luxury features like a pool or fire pit, you can charge more.

Rent out your car or parking space

If you don't use your car very often and it's just sitting in the driveway most of the day, rent it out! There's an app called Car Next Door which is a peer-to-peer car-sharing company. They provide all insurances and so on, and you can make enough money to offset the costs of owning the vehicle! And if you don't have a car but you have a parking space you're not using, you might be able to rent that out too, especially if it's in a prime location for city workers.

Rent out your house (or a room in your home)

With platforms such as Airbnb, you can rent out that spare room, granny flat or even your whole house. Airbnb is an online marketplace that allows people to rent out a space for short-term or holiday rentals. You can book just about any type of accommodation on Airbnb, from a spare room to a guest house, a backyard tent or even a boat. Accommodation is always in demand, and renting out a spare room – particularly if you live in an in-demand area – could net you a couple of hundred dollars per week, more if you're beachfront. Check out what other places in your area are going for, and how your potential rental space stacks up.

Ensure that the room or space is impeccably clean and decorated beautifully but simply. When people book an Airbnb space, they're looking for a place that is unique, rather than a cookie-cutter hotel room, so if you have some decorating skills, put them to use making the space interesting and fun. Invest in some excellent photography of your space before signing up to become a host. Hosts with professional photography tend to book 40% more than those who upload their own photographs. You also need to ensure you read all the terms and conditions before you get started, especially about any legal aspects.

As a host, it is your responsibility to equip the property with basic toiletries, cleaning essentials, towels and bed linen and anything else your guests might need. The little extra thoughtful touches, such as providing fresh milk and a packet of Tim Tams or a bottle of wine, are often the things that guests appreciate and might reward with better reviews.

How to price your space

Check Airbnb listings for your area (it's vital to check out your competition) to see what price comparable properties are renting for. Airbnb has an online calculator, which will help you come up with a price, too. Your goal is to get bookings and loads of positive reviews so that your listing becomes the most popular in your area and shows up the top in searches. You might consider renting your space at a lower price to start with in order to boost the number of stays and reviews you receive. Listing on Airbnb is free, but they do take a fee on a per-booking basis, which is determined by your pricing.

Rent out your caravan

Caravans are very expensive. If you own one that you only use occasionally, why not rent it out? Camplify is a peer-to-peer rental community that allows others to rent the use of your caravan rather than having to purchase one.

Become a house sitter

With many people choosing to have extended holidays and not wanting to leave their home unattended for lengthy periods of time, there is demand for people who can house sit. Some people prefer house sitters to live in the home, while others only require you to visit daily to walk and feed their pets or maintain the garden so there is the appearance of someone still living there – a great deterrent for would-be burglars.

You can approach this as a regular business opportunity, or look out for locations away from your home so you and the family can have a holiday in a new place while being paid to look after the home – it's like a reverse style of Airbnb!

Create profiles on any of the following:

- Mindahome
- Aussie House Sitters
- The House Sitters
- Happy House Sitters
- Trusted House Sitters

You will need to get hold of some great references and put your best case forward as to why you can be trusted to look after and respect someone's home. Of course, the more positive reviews you get on the platform you choose, the easier it will be to secure future work.

4.2 Create downloadable products

A whole other avenue of earning casually from home is to create products that other people pay to download. Downloadable products are online products that can be purchased from you and then delivered via your customer's email inbox or via a clickable link. They have been popular in the United States for years now, and they are really starting to take off here in Australia. As you're about to see, there are a whole range of options in this area, from one page to a whole book, from something that doesn't require a lot of creativity to much more in-depth projects.

The beauty of downloadable products is that once you have done the initial work, that's it – no postage required. People can buy your product at any time and the whole process of getting the item to their inbox is automated.

Downloadable products can include:

- E-courses
- Printables, templates and forms
- Ebooks

E-courses

E-courses are courses on a particular topic that you pay to watch online or download to work through at your own pace. They can be in the style of a lecture, or they can involve lessons and exercises that you work through. If you're knowledgeable in the field you are working in and find that people come to you for tips and information on the industry, consider creating an e-course on the topic that you can sell rather than give that information away for free!

Write or film all the content and structure it into easy to follow modules ready to be uploaded.

Some reputable e-course platforms include:

- Thinkific
- Teachable
- Udemy
- Podia
- LearnDash
- Skillshare

How much you can expect to make depends on the demand for your content, how in-depth your course is and how many people are willing to buy it. But the great thing about selling online courses is that once your course is done and available, you can keep selling the same content over and over again.

Printables, templates and forms

Printables, templates and forms are documents that you sell for people to download and print. There is some overlap between these, so I'll describe each in more detail.

Printables

Printables are generally single-page content that the customer prints (and sometimes laminates) and are usually family-oriented, time-saving information. If you're handy with design and have a good idea for something organisational, perhaps you can put the two together and create your own printables.

Printables can be things like:

- Weekly meal planner
- Shopping list
- Contact list
- Password tracker
- Cleaning checklist
- Holiday packing checklist
- Birthday and anniversaries list
- Family chore chart
- Printable wall art

There are heaps of printables available on platforms like Etsy to check out and put your own spin on. I highly recommend branding any printables you make with your name or a logo you create so that people remember where they bought it and come back for more.

Templates

Many clever graphic designers (and clever people in general) are now putting together fully branded kits and template packages to make it easy for individuals and businesses to get stuff done. They can just buy the template package and literally fill in the blanks rather than doing all the work from scratch. Customers pick the style they want, and usually they can order small changes to be made to reflect their brand. You, the designer, create the package, and it's all delivered to your client's inbox.

Template packages are cheaper than hiring a designer to do the work, but are certainly more expensive than other downloadables mentioned in this chapter. However, people are willing to pay for professional-looking, useful resources. They can be sold on your own website or through platforms like Etsy.

Invitations

Are you a seasoned pro at designing invitations for birthdays, weddings, events and other important occasions? You could not only sell templates as discussed but organise the printing too. If you already have a computer and a printer at home, you can cater for small jobs at first then upgrade your equipment or outsource to printing companies as you gain more clients. Advertise your work on Facebook, or create an Insta-gram account solely for work. Don't just think weddings and birthdays, think BIG!

Forms

Do you have a knack for creating simple and straightforward forms? The people who run small businesses, schools, childcare centres (the list goes on) don't always have time to create the forms they need to do their jobs – that's where you come in! You can create online forms and sample contracts that can be purchased and downloaded from platforms such as Etsy and then customised.

Types of forms include:
- Downloadable invoice
- Emergency contact list
- Shopping list (customisable)
- Order form
- Meal planning spreadsheet
- Spending tracker
- Budgeting spreadsheet

4.3 Ebooks

If you want to try your hand at writing a book, ebooks are a great thing to sell online. They are one of the most popular downloadable products. Think about it: you only have to write an ebook once. Then you sell copies of the digital file again and again and again – no physical stock to pay for, no postage. They can be sold worldwide and even translated into other languages. Another huge advantage of ebooks is that the selling process can be totally automated. Once you've done the hard work, you can just sit back and let the profits come in . . . Well, in theory! Best of all, ebooks can be created for very little cost if you do it all yourself. But you have to look at how to market your ebook so that you get sales. One way is to offer a free short sampler – this will help readers figure out if they want to pay to read more.

Advantages of ebooks over print books include:

- Searchable words or phrases within the document.
- Ebooks are environmentally friendly – no trees are cut down.
- Ebooks are easily accessible to the reader without the need for expensive design that a print book might attract.
- Ebooks can be a great tool for marketers to bring traffic to a website.
- Ebooks can contain links to audio, video or websites for further information, which is particularly useful if it's a how-to manual.

If you're really creative, you could try writing a novel. But for the rest of us, non-fiction is the easiest way to get started.

How to create a non-fiction ebook from start to finish

Step 1: Decide on a topic

If you can think of a topic, there will be a book, ebook or website on that subject – and there will be customers looking for ebooks on that topic. However, there are some niches that sell better than others. Here are some popular topics.

Family life ideas		
Teenagers	Teething	Feeding babies
Babies – first six weeks	Pocket money	Divorce and separation
Love and relationships	Pets	Baby-led weaning
Breastfeeding for beginners	Introducing vegetables to toddlers	Social anxiety for teenagers
Small business ideas		
How to write an ebook	How to start a business	Tax rules for small-business accounting
Understanding SEO	Marketing online	How to become a virtual assistant
Home ideas		
Home decor tips	Landscaping a new garden	Decorating on a budget
Knitting for beginners	Hobbies	Homemade Christmas gift guide
Tips for selling your home	Growing fruit trees	How to raise chickens
Repairs ideas		
Essential guide to sewing repairs	How to fix a hole in the wall	How to clean your hard drive
DIY home repair hacks	Repair it or chuck it?	Installing a motor
Toys and games ideas		
How to modify a nerf gun	Player's guide to Monopoly	How to win at chess
Gaming guide	Sudoku for students	Word games for kids
Cooking ideas		
Slow cooker meals	How to decorate cakes	Keto recipes

Gluten free living	Allergy cookbook	Christmas ebooks
Cooking for large families	Living dairy free	Switching to gluten free
Other great categories to try		
Biographies	Historical books	Self-improvement
Romance	True crime	Erotica
Law	Humour	Horror
Fantasy	Kids' books	Memoir

Step 2: Choose a program to make your ebook

This seems to be where people get stuck when wanting to create an ebook. But you can use Word, Google Docs or any other word processing format you like. As long as you can write the content and export the file as a PDF, you can use it. Sure, there are specific programs out there that will create fancy-looking ebooks, but before going to that type of expense, dip your toe in first to see if your ebook will make money.

Hot tip: When trying a new earning strategy, use as little money as possible to test that your idea works. If it does, look at putting more funds or time into it. If it doesn't, move on and try something else. Many people get stuck buying the biggest and best in the beginning before having a proven business model.

If you are planning to sell your ebook on platforms such as Amazon or Lulu, you may be required to use a specific type of formatting. Don't let this discourage you – most of these platforms have user manuals or step-by-step instructions on how to convert your online document to their requirements. Start by writing the content and figure the rest out as you need to.

Step 3: Writing the outline and body of your ebook

The next step is to spend time researching the topic and putting together a chapter outline. The outline of your ebook is where you decide what sort of information you need to include before you start writing. It also gives the book a clear introduction, body and conclusion, which summarises your main points and then lists your sources.

Think about what your readers will be looking for in your ebook, and design it to suit. I highly recommend using a spreadsheet to do this so you can add in chapters as they occur to you and to ensure you don't miss anything integral. If you aren't sure what chapter some information falls under, set it aside and either create a chapter to make it fit, or keep it to work into an existing chapter later on.

The next part is the actual writing of the ebook. Start working through the book, chapter by chapter, and write about each topic you listed in your outline using language that you would use if you were telling a stranger about the topic. Ebooks are all about simplicity, so you can usually use a more casual, conversational style of writing. Keep it as short and simple as you can – a lot of successful ebooks are as short as 30 pages.

If you get stuck on a chapter and become frustrated that you just can't get out what you are trying to say, don't force it. Save your work, go onto another chapter and come back to it later.

If you want to get an ebook out and for sale, you need to put aside time every single day to do some writing. Even when you don't feel like it, there are parts of your ebook that you can still do.

Step 4: Editing, formatting and polishing your ebook

Once you're happy with the writing you've done, the next step is to make your ebook ready for sale. This part often takes longer than actually writing the ebook!

Run a spellcheck over your work, then ensure that you go through it slowly, page by page, reading it out loud. If grammar and spelling is not your strong suit, have a detail-oriented friend read over it and highlight any areas that need improvement, or consider having it professionally edited and proofread.

> **Hot tip:** Grammarly is a useful grammar and spell-checking program to have on hand.

The next step is to add the extra features that will make your ebook unique and attractive to the audience. Add any images you might need by taking your own photos or finding free or cheap stock images (never, ever steal other people's images).

Some good stock image sites in which you can enter keyword searches include:
- Shutterstock
- iStock
- Bigstock
- Adobe Stock

Some free stock image sites (note that you may need to check the licence details for commercial use) include:
- Pexels
- StockSnap
- Unsplash
- Pixabay
- Gratisography
- Freestocks
- Stockvault
- Rawpixel
- Reshot
- picjumbo

Other items to make your ebook professional include:
- Page numbering
- Headers and footers
- Table of contents

Most word processors will have these functions. Again, if you're not really computer savvy, it may pay to get it professionally designed by someone who knows all the tricks!

Step 5: Create a fantastic cover

People do judge a book by the cover. You need a front cover that encourages a reader to be so keen to know more that they'll buy your ebook!

Tips for a fantastic cover:

- Keep it simple and to the point.
- Keep text to just the title of the ebook and your name.
- Choose an image or graphic that accurately gets across to your customers what the ebook is about.

Remember that when people are browsing the covers of ebooks online, the thumbnail image of the ebook is very small. So complicated images or highly detailed designs are just not going to grab people's attention. You also have to consider what will appeal to your customers. For example, if you are writing a book about make-up and beauty, the front cover should look a lot more expensive and luxe than, say, an ebook about how to start a home compost system.

You also have to consider your very own branding. Will you be doing a whole range of ebooks in a similar vein? Do you have a brand or logo already? Perhaps you want to use a consistent cover font across your series of ebooks?

Great platforms for designing an ebook cover include:

- Canva
- PicMonkey
- Designrr

Step 6: Where to sell your ebook

Okay, so your ebook is finished. It is edited, thoroughly checked and boasts a fantastic front cover – now it's time to make some money! That means getting it to your customers. If you don't have your own website, don't worry – there are plenty of platforms available where you can sell your ebook, although they usually take a commission on sale.

Some popular platforms for ebooks include:

- Lulu
- ClickBank
- Amazon's Kindle Direct Publishing
- Barnes & Noble Press
- Smashwords
- Payhip
- Blurb
- PayLoadz
- E-junkie
- BookBaby
- Scribd
- Tradebit
- Kobo Writing Life
- PaySpree
- Ecwid
- Feiyr
- ManyBooks

For quite a few of these platforms, you need to convert your ebook into a PDF format. To do that, just use the Save As option in your word processing program and choose the PDF option. Save the file, then upload it. Some platforms also require you to upload your file into another type of format, so read the instructions carefully and follow them. Amazon is quite particular about how each ebook is formatted, but don't let this dissuade you from using it – just be patient and follow the directions.

Step 7: Pricing your ebook for market

Pricing your ebook can be tricky. Have a look at the prices of other ebooks in the same category and use this as a guide. Think about how much information you've included, the ebook's length, and the demand for your topic. I've seen ebooks that are free and I've seen ebooks that cost up to $200 (the really expensive ones are usually medical or engineering texts). You want to price your ebook low enough that people are willing to buy it, but not so low that you don't earn decent money.

If you are selling the book directly through a platform like Shopify, you can afford to keep the price low as you pocket 100% of the sale price. However, other selling platforms may take as much as 30% commission. In that case, you'll need to add that 30% on top of the price so that you still get the remuneration you want for your work. Remember, you can price your ebook differently for different platforms!

As a general rule, the higher the demand for your ebook, and the more you have published in the past, the more you can charge.

Step 8: Marketing your ebook

Now that you've done the hard work in writing and publishing the ebook, you need people to actually buy it – this is where marketing comes in. To get customers to buy, you need them to find your ebook. This doesn't mean you need to spend a fortune on marketing – in fact, you can get away with spending nothing – but you still need to put in the time. Here are a few ideas to get the ball rolling.

Set up social media channels for promotion

As an author, you should have your own (business, not personal) Facebook page, Instagram account and others if you want. See section 9.2 where I talk about the different social media channels. Promote your book on all these channels – while you're promoting the book, you're also promoting yourself!

Give away a few copies for review

Many people are more willing to purchase after reading positive reviews online. So consider sending the ebook to a few people in exchange for them leaving you a truthful review afterwards. If you can get someone popular, well-known or authoritative in the industry to review it, that's an added bonus.

Record a video

Record a heartfelt video (even just recorded on your phone is fine) that you can upload to your social media channels. Uploading videos on YouTube can be a good alternative to having a website – it can be a way to attract new readers/audience to your ebook. Ask your friends and family to share the video so you reach more people.

Approach influencers to review or sell your ebook

If someone you know already has a public profile, they may be willing to post about your ebook on their social media. They may also have an online store where they sell various items. If you think your ebook could be a good fit with their profile, you can ask them if they would be interested in selling the ebook to their audience, offering to pay them a commission on sales.

Offer others a commission for sales

If you are lucky enough to have a website or a Shopify account, you can set up an affiliate program where other people can choose to sell your product for a commission. If you don't have your own platform, you can still approach people with websites to sell your ebook for a commission. When setting a fair price for their commission, make sure you take into consideration that they are processing the payment, paying any GST and dealing with customers – your commission needs to reflect all this work that they're doing to sell the product for you. For ebooks, I think a fair commission would be 40–50% of the retail price you've set.

The most common mistakes made by ebook sellers

Many people write ebooks, then complain that their ebook doesn't sell. 'What a waste of time,' they say. 'I've done all this work for nothing.'

That's why marketing is such an important part of the ebook business model. It is crucial to inject the same amount of energy into marketing your ebook as you did writing it. Here are some of the most common mistakes made by ebook sellers.

Writing on unfamiliar topics
People buy ebooks to gain knowledge they don't already have on a topic. If you're not sure about the topic you are writing about, that will come through in the writing! Stick to what you know, or risk getting bad reviews – and bad reviews don't help sell books.

Starting but not finishing
This is a really common problem. The thing is, you can't be successful if you don't finish your ebook! So how do you solve this? There are many productivity tools and strategies you can consider, but one simple way is to set a goal to complete one chapter heading per day until you slowly tick them all off. Another great one is to find an accountability partner so you keep up the writing.

Using a white label version of an ebook without changing the words
A white label ebook is a generic product you can buy in order to rebrand and resell as your own. Now, that may sound incredible, but it's a real thing people do. The problem is that there are thousands of people doing just that and selling the very same copy of a very publicly available ebook. This means the market in a given area can be saturated already – some people don't even change the front cover!

If you choose to go down the white label route, make sure you rewrite the content in your own words – and please redo the cover. By rewriting the book, you turn it into your own product – it's just a way to get a head start.

The ebook is awesome, but no one is buying it
Have you put your ebook for sale on all the available platforms? Does it have an eye-catching front cover? Is it priced correctly? Is your

sales copy enticing enough to make customers want to buy? Have you displayed glowing reviews in your sales copy? Do you *have* sales copy? If not, read on!

How to write killer sales copy

Sales copy is the write-up about your ebook that you use to persuade people to purchase it (this applies to other sorts of products you might sell too). Your copy needs to be short, snappy, informative and to the point. Good sales copy tells your consumer how they will benefit from your product, why it's made for them, and all the ways it will make their life better or easier.

To write great sales copy, step into the buyer's shoes. In order to write great sales copy, step into the buyers' psyche – imagine their needs, wants and desires. Show how purchasing your ebook might help meet their needs.

Another trick for writing compelling sales copy is to share your story about how the ebook came about. Have you been in the same position as possible buyers? Think back to what made you write about that topic, and share your real-life situation.

Keep your sales copy to a maximum of two paragraphs and have multiple images of your ebook.

Now, writing a sales pitch is *hard*. I'm not pretending that it isn't tough – in fact, I still find it really difficult. Sometimes it takes another person to read the book and tell you why they liked it! Jot down exactly what they say and use that in your copy.

Some further tips to help you write killer sales copy:

- Look at how other books are pitched. Note what you like or dislike about the pitches.
- If you have a friend or contact in the advertising business, ask them to look at your pitch and give you some feedback.
- Explain how your book will solve your consumers' problems.
- Include a clear call to action; that is, how to buy.
- Spell out the benefits of your ebook or why it's different from others.

- Don't be wishy-washy – use direct language that is straight to the point.
- Try this industry formula for writing sales pitches for books: the situation, the problem, promise a twist, emphasise the mood, tell them what you want.
- Don't give away the whole ebook in your sales pitch. You need buyers to purchase. Keep them guessing.
- 150 words is plenty.
- Write simply and clearly enough that a 10-year-old can understand what you're saying.

What to do if your ebook is still not selling

Don't give up! Send your ebook to some friends or family and ask for constructive criticism. Make improvements to your sales copy, or the front cover to see if it does any better. Try out a different front cover for a short period of time to see if it helps.

Get exposure. If you haven't done this already, send emails out to influencers and websites asking them to review your ebook. Ask influencers to become sellers in exchange for a good commission.

If you do have a bit of a budget, consider creating a landing page (that is, a single-page website) specifically for your ebook – it works well as people find it when they use search terms related to your topic. See sections 8.3 and 10.3 for more about websites.

Creating and selling ebooks can be very lucrative if you're willing to put in the hard work. Just remember that marketing is probably the most important tool you have.

4.4 Freelancing

Freelancing is a fantastic job to do from home because you choose your jobs and your hours. You can do the occasional job or take on repeat clients who want work done every week. Freelancing is particularly good for people who have professional or office qualifications. You might find yourself developing your skills so much you decide to structure your work as a business instead of a side job.

Here are some freelancing ideas:

- Graphic design
- Photo editing
- Video creation or editing
- Grant writing
- Travel consulting
- Web design
- Teaching
- Data entry
- Transcribing
- Information technology
- Writing
- Photography
- SEO services
- Event coordinating
- Bookkeeping
- Editing
- Social media marketing
- Virtual assistant

Getting started

If you want to see if freelancing is for you, you might start small by offering your services on these sites.

Freelancer is your one-stop shop for finding work in many areas – graphic artist, social media manager, you name it. This is the perfect place to go and look for online work right away. The site posts jobs (for example, writing a business plan for a start-up, writing an article for a newspaper, designing an Excel spreadsheet, etc.) and you submit how much you want to be paid for the job and the time frame you can get it done in. You'll be competing with people worldwide to get that job, but it doesn't necessarily come down to who offers the lowest rate – potential employers will also check out your rating (something you will build in time) and feedback to evaluate your value for money.

Fiverr is a marketplace for digital services online. To make money on Fiverr, you sign up and advertise your skills. Whether you're savvy with WordPress, can design apps, are a gun at video editing or write sharp copy, Fiverr can be a great way to pick up a bit of work online. When this site first started, all jobs were only $5 so it wasn't a great way to make money, but now it's open to every budget – no need to undercharge for your skills.

99designs is a contest-based business that matches designers and illustrators with clients. So if you're an artist or graphic designer or just like to draw, you can bid for different jobs and have your artwork used on a commercial basis.

Upwork is an online platform that connects a wide range of freelancers with potential clients. Jobs are posted by clients, then you can apply to do that job and post the fee you require. This is a great place to get decent, consistent online work.

Freelance writing

If you love writing, becoming a freelance writer is a great way for a mum to earn at home. Your can fit your writing around caring for the family, it's a great challenge, and when you see something you've written out there and published, you'll really feel good about yourself.

You don't need fancy tools to become a freelance writer, but if you haven't had much experience with using Microsoft Word, Google Workspace or any editing software, it's a good idea to look into a course to brush up on some basic skills – check with your local council or find an online course.

Websites are looking for great writers all the time because they need fresh content on a regular basis. As well as articles, websites are often looking for poetry, short stories, essays, recipes, interviews and vlogs.

Choose your strength, and then approach the websites that will accept your material. I'm going to focus on writing articles, as that's the most common form of work around.

Just keep in mind that freelance writers often start out earning near on nothing for their work until they build up a solid reputation. It can be slow going working your way up to a viable income. You can be on very strict deadlines, which can be hard when you're at home with a sick baby or a demanding toddler, so think carefully before signing up for an assignment. If you miss your deadline, you're unlikely to be asked to write for that site again.

If you get knocked back on your first few goes, don't give up! Concentrate on your writing skills and check that you have followed the submission instructions to the letter. Remember, what one website may reject, another will accept – so apply to many. Keep trying and build up your skill set.

Websites to try

The following websites are places you can join for free and list your services. You can also approach websites or publications with examples of your writing to see if they are willing to give you a go. Standard rates for writing for a website in Australia start from around $20 per article for an inexperienced beginner through to $250 for a researched article with photographs.

iWriter

iWriter is a very easy-to-use website that allows you to get started on your writing career right away. Payment will be small at first, but as you get good feedback from customers, you can increase your rate. Professional writers who have submitted over 30 pieces of content can command up to $200 an article.

Listverse

Listverse is a terrific website that has a Top 10 of Everything. They pay $100 for every published article.

Stay at Home Mum
This site (my site) accepts guest posts. If we publish the article we'll pay you between $30 and $150 per post depending on suitability, length and subject.

Freelance Mom
The Freelance Mom accepts guest posts and pays between $75 and $100 per post. There is a strict submission policy, but it's all laid out for you before you send in your work.

Upwork
This site also features writing jobs. Sign up and then browse this site for jobs – they will state exactly how much they are paying and what they're looking for.

Tips for getting your articles accepted

Ensure you read through all the rules and stipulations *before* submitting an article. As an website editor myself, nothing makes me madder than receiving an article that doesn't meet the brief I've diligently written out. So remember:

- Stick to the specified word count.
- Stick to the requested topic.
- Ensure the topic hasn't already been covered on the website you're writing for.
- Stick to your strengths – write on the topics you most enjoy.
- Check your spelling and grammar.
- Read the submission guidelines carefully.
- Don't forget to include a bio for yourself, including a picture.

Writing grant proposals

Most small businesses don't have the time or knowledge to apply for the many and varied grants available, which would otherwise be a fantastic asset to the business.

If you have a background in professional writing, government employment or journalism, writing grant proposals for others would suit you well. Most grant writers work on a freelance basis so look at places like Upwork. You can set your rate for each proposal or choose an hourly fee.

Conclusion

There are so many ways you can earn at home without having to go to the lengths of setting up your own full-on business. Dip your toe in and you might be surprised by the results. Many of these ways to earn money online require patience and persistence, so don't give up! That said, if an idea isn't working out, there's no harm in trying something new. If you find an area you succeed in, you can build on it to grow your earnings and maybe even develop it into a business.

Chapter 5

Casual earning offline

We all have great skills that we've honed over the years. As we've seen, if you have an area of expertise, you can harness the power of your mind to make money from home. But perhaps you don't relish being 'connected' all day (that is, staring at a screen), or you have creative skills that lend themselves to more practical expression. Great! There are many ways you can make money offline, with the internet as merely a support for your work rather than central to it.

What do I mean? Think posting a beautiful Instagram pic of your succulents for sale, or finding clients for your home salon via your local Facebook page. Have you mastered playing a musical instrument? You can teach beginners how to learn that instrument, or play at weddings on the weekend. Are you a baking whiz, with plenty of themed parties under your belt? How about advertising your services baking personalised cakes, biscuits and party fare? Are you known as a bit of a wordsmith or a whiz with numbers? You can become a tutor for students or people who have English as their second language.

5.1 Offline job ideas

Let's look at some specific examples in more detail – perhaps some will mesh with your interests and skills.

Bartending for parties and events

If you're over 18 and have a knack for mixing drinks, why not offer your services as a bartender for catering events and private parties? Bartending in this context usually includes coming up with a drinks menu that the client agrees to, preordering the alcohol and having equipment organised, enough ice and garnishes all cut up ready to go. You will be expected to look the part (for example, plain black or black pants and a white shirt) and have good people skills.

All that's required for bartending anywhere in Australia is an RSA (Responsible Service of Alcohol) certificate – it's a one-day course in person, or self-paced online. A good bartender can earn up to $500 for an evening of mixing.

Personal concierge

The world we live in is busier than ever and many people working long hours just don't have time to do errands needed for the home and family. That's where a personal concierge comes in handy. You can make yourself available to pick up the drycleaning, do the food shopping or pick up and drop off the kids at school.

You will need a driver's licence, a Blue Card or Working With Children Check, no criminal record and a reliable car.

Advertise your services on local noticeboards and in Facebook groups, and this is a great one for word of mouth. If people are happy with your services, they'll recommend you!

You can expect to make upwards of $20 per hour.

Mystery shopper

A mystery shopper is a person assigned by an agency to go to a particular shop and critique the customer service given by that store. It is invaluable for larger chains to see if their staff are doing their job correctly or to locate a potential problem. You need to do the mystery shop 'undercover' and retain all the information gathered on the mission (such as the salesperson's name, how they greeted you, how long it took to be served and so on), write it all up in a detailed report and submit back to the agency, usually within a 24-hour period.

Mystery shoppers don't make a whole lot. You can expect to be paid about $20 per job, plus a reimbursement of any purchases made in the store (with a proven receipt, of course). Some stores offer no money at all, but a voucher for the shop instead. However, if you are a mum at home and you regularly go to the shops anyway, it's a good way to earn a little extra. Plus, it is kinda fun!

Some agencies request that you don't take friends or children along with you, so if your kids aren't in school or childcare and you don't have a regular babysitter, this may not work for you.

Tutor

If you were good at school and you're super patient, then tutoring is a terrific idea. You can work the hours that suit you, and you'll be making a difference in the life of a child or adult. There are even online tutoring companies around now, so you can work from home. Experience in teaching is definitely a plus, as is a qualification in your subject. The two things you'll absolutely need is passion for both your subject and for teaching kids and the patience of a saint.

Tell everyone you know what you're offering and they can recommend your services to people in need. You might also approach some local schools to see if they'll recommend you to potential clients or advertise your services in their newsletter or similar. Once you get a couple of clients, you may find that word of mouth is enough to attract more clients, or you can create a dedicated Facebook page to advertise your services.

What you will need to start:
- Blue Card or Working With Children Check, depending on which state you're in

I know we're in the offline earning section of this book, but a lot of tutoring can also be done online (especially at the time of writing, during the COVID-19 pandemic). If you're going to operate online rather than face-to-face, you'll need:

- A reliable computer and internet connection
- Microphone and camera
- A video-conferencing program with screen-sharing feature

Rather than sourcing your own clients, you could also consider joining established online tutoring companies such as:

- Kip McGrath
- Cluey Learning
- MathsOnline

Uber driver

Being an Uber driver (or a driver for another app that offers a similar service, such as Shebah, which is for women) means you can choose your own hours – great for mums. The more you drive, the more money you make. Provided you're at least 21 years old, all you'll need to start is a valid driver's licence, completed background check, a reliable car that's up to Uber's standards, a smartphone and an Uber account.

The pros of Uber driving is that you can work during school hours or around your current obligations, you get to meet lots of people and you can work more if you need more money.

The cons include wear and tear on your vehicle and potentially having to deal with drunk or obnoxious passengers. The supplemental Uber insurance coverage can be quite expensive, too.

Knitting classes

Knitting is huge these days, and although YouTube classes are great for reminding people of the basics, personalised instruction can be much more effective in getting new knitters started, or for those going next-level. You could run beginners' classes on making popular small projects such as baby beanies, or offer instruction on advanced techniques such as stranded knitting or different ways to turn a sock heel.

You could make from $50 per person for a two-hour class, more if you also supply the yarn and needles. If you need a venue, reach out to your local yarn store (or even local library) – the store might take a cut, or it might provide the space for free if the students need to buy materials there.

Upcycle second-hand or vintage furniture

Are you into upcycling old furniture? If you have an interest in interior designing and making the old new again, then you can definitely make money out of it. Upcycling is a skill and practising will make you better. Start with simple and basic styles, such as cleaning and painting wooden furniture. Once you're confident in doing the basics, then you can learn more of those complicated techniques such as restoration and reupholstery. You will magically add value to the pieces you work on, making it a great and satisfying way to make a profit as well as keeping you occupied as you work on each piece.

Purchase pieces of furniture from Ebay or local buy, swap and sell pages. An easy way to get started is to buy a few pots of chalk paint. This paint is brilliant because you don't need to sand the furniture first, just give it a coat, sand, then add a waxy coat over the top – and your furniture goes from drab to fab! You can purchase chalk paint from most hardware stores.

You can look at selling your furniture at local markets or Facebook Marketplace, Etsy, eBay or Gumtree; advertise in your local newsletters or even approach furniture stores in your area to see if they will sell your products on commission.

Grow and sell plants for resale

If you are a budding (excuse the pun!) gardener, you could grow seedlings and look at selling them at your local market or online. All you need are some pots, good quality soil, fertiliser, a bit of outdoor space and patience. Succulents are huge at the moment and they are really easy to grow, so why not cash in on the trend?

Great plants to consider selling:
- Vegetable seedlings
- Herbs

- Potted flowers in hanging baskets
- Groundcovers
- Indoor plants
- Succulents

Various food-related businesses

A word to the wise here: most of these food-related ideas require you to have access to a commercial kitchen and might require you getting a food-safety or food-handling certificate or licence. Always check the legal requirements in your state or territory before selling food or consumables that you've made yourself.

Picnic baskets

Capitalise on your well-honed mum skills of putting together lunches on the run by starting a picnic basket business. Whether you're packing a picnic basket for a romantic date or for a day out on the green, or a kid's birthday picnic, you can make a name for yourself by packing local fresh produce that can be enjoyed out in nature. These would also be great for a movie night.

Think of a menu that can be put into a basket and transported easily. There are so many delicious picnic-friendly foods to come up with.

What to charge will really depend on the contents. Taking your time and the cost of food into consideration, you should at least double the cost. Invest in some low-cost picnic baskets, and ask that they be returned after they're finished with. You'll need to provide cutlery, plates, cups and napkins as you want your basket to provide maximum convenience.

Pie making

If you can make a really great tasty pie that people rave about, consider making your pies to sell at markets or to anyone who wants them. You can charge as much as $80 per pie depending on the size and ingredients.

Freshly pureed baby food

If your baby absolutely loves the range of fresh purees and baby food you make, why not look at making it for others? Just selling to friends and family will cover your costs, but you never know, you could end up selling it on a commercial basis to supermarkets for megadollars.

Cheese platters

There are so many beautiful gourmet cheeses around now – plus dairy-free cheeses have become very popular. Why not look at putting together platters for sale? You could also do a cheese subscription box or provide little plates of various cheeses at functions as nibbles.

A gourmet cheese platter can start at $50.

Coffee

Everyone loves coffee. If you can run a machine and make it mobile, you can sell coffee at markets, weddings and other functions. There is a trend to have tiny caravans that you can tow around – sure, that's a bit of an expensive start-up cost on top of your espresso machine, but look how adorable they are!

The sky's the limit on how much you might make – if your barista skills are great and you're the only coffee around, you could rake it in.

Fairy floss

Make delicious fresh fairy floss at school fetes, local markets and carnivals with a stall. A relatively inexpensive fairy floss machine, ingredients and wooden sticks are pretty much all you need! You can pick up commercial fairy floss machines for under $300.

Flavoured olive oils

Just about all home cooks use olive oil, with many indulging in the small variety of flavoured olive oils available – what about a bespoke range of flavoured oils? It's quite easy – it's just a matter of purchasing high grade olive oil, infusing it with flavour through herbs or aromatics, and letting time do its thing. Then you need to think about food-safe bottling and labelling. Sell your flavoured olive oils at markets or online.

5.2 Start a market stall

Do you sew, bake or create unique crafts, treats or gifts that you would like to sell? Then why not take the plunge and apply for a stall at your local market? Markets are generally held on the weekends, either in the morning or for the entire day. You will need to register your stall and product with the market administration, which can be done in person, online or through an application form, depending on what market you are attending.

It is actually relatively easy to get involved in selling your products through the local markets. It's a great way to get your name out there and have some fun doing it. You can try your local farmers market to start with, but there are also markets specialising in, for example, babies or craft and handmade items.

Below is a quick guideline to what you will need.

Products

First things first – you need something to actually sell. Make sure you have enough items to fill up a table. Whether you make your product yourself, import it or on-sell, have a wide selection and a little of everything.

Here are some of the most popular items to sell at a local market.

Food ideas		
Baked goods such as cakes, cookies, slices, fresh breads, pies and pastries	Coffee caravan	Farm-grown fruit and vegetables
Hot breakfast (something customers can hold while they walk)	Ice cream and milkshakes	Flavoured olive oils

Spice blends	Burgers and hot dogs	Uniquely flavoured coffee beans
Handmade chocolates or confectionery	Homemade chutneys, sauces and relishes	Freshly made lemonade
Unique flavoured popcorn or nuts	Fresh eggs (chicken, duck)	Pet treats
Homemade fudge	Fresh yoghurt or cheese	Kombucha or kefir
Other ideas		
Plants, including vegetable seedlings or heirloom fruit and vegetable seeds	Handmade jewellery, including resin jewellery	Bath and beauty products, such as soaps, scrubs and bath bombs
Vintage goods	Unique handbags	Organic cleaning products
Kids' costumes	Handmade baby products (bibs, onesies, pyjamas)	Hanging baskets
Second-hand clothing	Bric-a-brac	Handmade clothing or aprons
Fairy gardens	Scented candles	Leather bookmarks
Market services		
Barber or hairdressing stand	Head and shoulder massage	Tattooist

All market stall owners selling consumable food products are required to have a temporary food stall licence, which is available from your local council. All foodstuffs must comply with the Food Standards Code to ensure that the food you supply is safe and suitable for people to eat.

Foodstuffs are also required to be labelled correctly, stating all the ingredients in case of allergies. Ensure you check the business.gov.au website for the most updated information on food labelling requirements in your state or territory.

Display

For a great market stall, you will need a way to display your items. You may wish to get gift boxes or gift bags to display the products. You can buy jewellery displays, coathangers, brochure displays, mannequins and heads, and all other types of displays online, or you can think outside the box and look around the house for spare boxes, containers and other items that may work just as well.

Hot tip: Always have business cards available with your contact details on your display table – you never know what business you could get outside the markets.

Gazebo or shade cover

In order to protect your customers and your products, it's a good idea to invest in a pop-up gazebo. Aim for one measuring around 3 x 3 metres. You can expect to pay around $100 to $250 new for one of these.

Trestle table

A trestle table gives you a place to display your products. You can pick up a cheap folding one at places like Kmart for around $70, or at any camping or hardware store. Cover it with a colourful tablecloth that complements your display and products.

Some markets allow you to hire a table for the duration.

Signage

Always have the name of your business prominently displayed. Ensure you have a matching Facebook page and Instagram so that people know where to go to find out more about your business – and to possibly buy items outside the markets. Keep your signage simple and to the point.

Sales

You need to have a way to keep track of your sales. People are less likely to carry cash these days, so you might look into getting an EFTPOS machine – they are much cheaper than they used to be. Make sure you have enough cash and change to meet the needs of your customers. You don't need a cash register, unless you have one lying around – a lockable tin box will do the job.

Market trading insurance

You'll require insurance including public liability and product liability insurance for your stall and the products you sell. Called 'market trading insurance', most of these policies are fairly easy to obtain online. You can go through some of the main insurance companies out there, such as AAMI. You can expect to pay a few hundred dollars per year for public liability insurance. This will protect you in the event of a death or accident from your products. Your market host can also help you with good insurance providers – don't be shy in asking them for a recommendation.

Other nifty market hints

If you have access to an iPad or similar tablet, it's worth putting a little sign on your stall that you are collecting email addresses for people interested in your product or service. You can use a newsletter system such as Mailchimp to send out information on new products or market locations to interested customers.

Ensure you take photos of your stall or your customers (with their permission) to post on your social media channels. This makes your stall easily identifiable.

Look after yourself during the market day – wear comfortable shoes, take plenty of water, ensure your phone is charged (but don't sit there with eyes glued to your phone during the market) and have snacks on hand. See if a family member or friend can come and give you a hand or cover you during a bathroom break.

Remember to smile, have fun, and never do the hard sell thing – people don't like it. Let your product shine. Finally, the biggest thing you need is the desire to do it. If you've always wanted to try something like this, then now you know exactly how!

Conclusion

As you can see, the potential for casual work you can do offline is enormous. You might find something that gels perfectly with your life-style and interests. If you develop a taste for something a little bigger, though, the next part of this book is for you – how to kickstart your own business!

Part 3

Creating your own business

Chapter 6

Are you suited to owning a business?

Your biggest strength is knowing your weakness.

Running a business is not for everyone. There are many people who are far better suited to a traditional paid employment model, or don't have the appetite for risk and hard work that starting a business can entail. If that describes you, the best thing you can do is acknowledge it. That's not to say that there aren't ways to make money at home without a business – there are, and the previous chapters cover some great ideas on that. But if you want to build something of your own, and hopefully make some real money, this part of the book is for you.

6.1 Do you have the drive, personality and appetite for risk?

Here's a shortlist of traits of people who have developed successful businesses from the ground up. A good business owner-to-be is willing to do these things:

- Work weekends, nights, holidays or all three to get your idea off the ground.
- Be a good problem solver.
- Always go the extra mile.
- Ask for help when you need it.

- Be tenacious.
- Put yourself out there.
- Take risks.
- Get out of your comfort zone.
- Be scared every single day.

Hmmm. Sounds appealing, huh? If you tick only a few of these boxes but are still keen to start a business, start listening to or reading about others' success stories. You will learn that nearly every entrepreneur who has made it had a huge series of setbacks and failures before they had success. Just because you aren't ready now, it doesn't mean you won't be in the future.

Not everyone is suited to owning a business. If you prefer a steady income that arrives in the bank every fortnight, scheduled holidays, being free on weekends and the security of a full-time position, then perhaps a business is not for you.

Similarly, you need to be starting your own business for the right reasons – not just because you struggle to work for other people, and want to be the master of your own destiny. If your heart isn't in your business, you're setting yourself up for failure from the very start.

You should also consider your personality type. The most successful businesspeople are self-starters who can decide on what they want and then do what it takes to make it happen.

And if you weigh it all up and accept that you're not someone who's compatible with running a business, that's not to say you can't look at other ways to secure more income – hell no! You still have options.

I won't sugar-coat this: starting a business is a risk. It is outside most people's comfort zones. But that's what makes it so rewarding!

Some of the responsibilities as a business owner include handling taxes such as GST if you are earning over a certain amount (check with the Australian Taxation Office for where you'll stand), covering yourself for superannuation, dealing with the expense of new business equipment or computer programs you need, and remembering that you really have no paid holidays.

If you are trading under your own name, you won't need to register your business name. However, if you have already thought of a wonderful name for your business, you will need to register this with ASIC (the Australian Securities and Investments Commission). This does incur a cost, but it is essential. You can also simply work under your own name and apply for an ABN, which is a very simple process. I'll talk about this more in Chapter 7.

6.2 A word on multi-level marketing schemes

If you want to start a business, I want you to succeed! But I don't want you to confuse starting your own business with getting in on a multi-level marketing scheme.

Good friends and family members don't constantly hassle you to join or buy something from the scheme they've been sucked into, or rant about an 'amazing business opportunity' at every social function. The only time you hear from them shouldn't be because they want to give you yet another mind-numbing sales pitch.

If you're guilty of this, I don't care if I've offended you. You've probably offended everyone you know.

Multi-level marketing, also known as MLMs, network marketing or direct selling, is where you join a program as a sales representative because they promised you things like 'financial freedom' and 'being your own boss' and lots of other stuff that might sound amazing if you're a stay-at-home mum looking for a way to make an income. Whatever the product is – essential oils, diet supplements, lingerie or make-up or nail foils – it's overwhelmingly likely that you're not going to make a lot of money from the sales you make. You'll be making money from a portion of the sales from the others you recruit into your 'down-line' and you, in turn, will be giving a portion of your sales to the person above you. The person at the top level is the one making most of the cash.

If you ask someone who is trying to recruit you into one of these schemes if it's a pyramid scheme, they'll be very quick to tell you exactly why it isn't one, and explain some very complex and official-sounding business structure to you. It's a clear case of the old 'baffle them with bullshit' sales technique.

Pyramid schemes are illegal, and while multi-level marketing is not illegal . . . in my opinion most are pretty dodgy. According to the Australian Competition and Consumer Commission, this is how you tell the difference between a genuine multi-level marketing scheme and a pyramid:

- Are the rewards purely based on product sales (by either themselves or others they introduce to the scheme)?
- Are the products genuine and of real value, and of a type that normally will be used and purchased time and time again by a consumer, and not at a grossly inflated price?

If you answer yes to both questions, it is likely that the scheme is considered a legitimate multi-level marketing scheme. This is where it gets confusing because of the 'real value' of the products being flogged at 'not a grossly inflated price'. How many times has someone you know tried to sell you something you're sceptical about the quality of and costs a freaking fortune? I'm talking to you, woman who tries to flog me herbal supplements that cost a packet per bottle, several times a year.

Stay-at-home mums are often the target of these schemes. Their desire to earn income to help the household budget out makes them a really good target for people looking to recruit others into their down-lines. But I am here to tell you, more often than not, you will bust your arse for very little return.

As well as being wary of *that* friend, also avoid the 'amazing opportunity to be your own boss' ads. You find them on legitimate job sites. Presumably they've run out of family and friends to annoy, or they're just expanding their horizons. They'll spam mum's groups on Facebook using a stock photo of someone lying on a beach with palm trees, making claims that you can have the 'lifestyle you always dreamed of' and 'create wealth' and all sorts of other wonderful promises.

Just like anyone with any ounce of wisdom ever said, 'If it's too good to be true, it probably is.' There are some genuine opportunities out there, but I caution you to *always* do your homework. Dig a little deeper than the fluffy marketing pitch being presented to you. Better now than after you have committed to this 'amazing opportunity' and you have to find a way out. They *never* reveal what the business actually is, of course, and they'll usually have a spammy email address for more information like amazing$ucce$$4u@hotmail.com. This should be your first clue that this person isn't a serious business person with a worthwhile opportunity. If it were, say, a major fast food chain looking for franchisees, they'd tell you as much and they'd have an email address that reflected their business name. The reason they don't reveal who they really are is because if they were truthful and said, 'This opportunity is to shill diet supplements on behalf of a company that Choice recently exposed as being dodgy,' you wouldn't bother applying, would you? If you respond to them, they will give you their sales pitch. And it's easier to rid an infested kindergarten of head lice than getting rid of these people once they have your contact details.

To try to get you on board, many of these fake business or so-called friends will turn to faux spiritual shit about how they are now on a journey to fulfil their destiny, and they couldn't have done it before they 'opened their minds to the possibilities'. You'll start to wonder if they're still trying to get you on board to sell some beauty products or diet pills, or are they recruiting you to a cult? It's really the same thing in many cases: cults also prey on vulnerable people to exploit them and make lots of empty promises. So, avoid these schemes and tactics like the plague! Phew!

6.3 So what's your big idea?

I'm betting that nearly 100% of people reading this right now have thought about different business ideas already – and they've been so overwhelmed with the steps that they've given up before they even really got started. If that describes you, don't worry – it's perfectly normal, and in fact shows your entrepreneurial spirit is already there!

My biggest piece of advice to people who are seeking a business idea and don't know where to start, is to sit back and look for a gap in the market. What's annoying or lacking for you or others that you may have a solution for? Is there something a business is currently doing that you know you could do better?

Try this method:

1. Grab a piece of paper. Draw up three different columns.
2. In the first column, write down all the things that you're good at. For example, if you're a data entry whiz or you love numbers, write that down. None of this has to make sense yet – just let it be a brainstorm of information. If I was writing this I'd put things like:
   - Typing
   - Writing
   - New ideas
   - Solving problems
3. In the second column, write down all the things you're interested in. What do you love hobby-wise? Again, I'll write a few ideas:
   - Fashion
   - Gardening
   - Holidays
   - Family genealogy
4. Now, in the third column, write down the things you don't like doing (probably the most important). Some examples are:
   - Cleaning
   - Filing
   - Accounts
   - Talking on the phone

Now you have a good start for getting an idea for your new business – something that fits within those three columns. Put the piece of paper somewhere you'll see it every single day, and you will find that you start noticing gaps in the market that fit in with your notes. Our brains are awesome like that – if you give them something specific to focus on, they can start to filter out the noise and highlight potential opportunities.

The problem with most business ideas is that they're overwhelming. They either require a large financial outlay that most people just don't have, or specialised skills that require study (which again requires finances), or the market is already flooded with similar endeavours.

I'm going to show you lots of business ideas that don't necessarily require these things. Money always helps, but if that's not available to you, it just means you need to put a lot of 'sweat equity' into your business.

Let's start by taking a detailed look at three very distinct business areas that could be a fantastic fit for many stay-at-home mums: becoming a virtual assistant, starting your own fashion line and selling subscription boxes. I'll cover more of the nitty-gritty of how to set yourself up, where to find work and how to promote your business, any tax considerations and business logistics. And you'll see that much of this can be applied to the many other business ideas that follow.

Virtual assistant

So many people who run their own businesses have no time to do the little nitty-gritty tasks that are essential to keeping on top of things. Virtual assistants are a cost-effective way for small business owners to get the help they need. It's the perfect job opportunity for stay-at-home mums. You can fit it in around your own responsibilities and it's a great way to learn a lot of different skills that you can apply to other areas of work in the future.

There are a few essentials that you will need to have before you even start advertising for work:

- A reliable computer with at least 50GB of memory space to allow for uploading and downloading of documents
- A decent internet connection
- A word processing program such as Microsoft Word or G Suite
- A spreadsheet program such as Excel or Google Spreadsheets
- A colour printer

- Cloud storage such as Dropbox
- Public liability insurance
- An email address that you check regularly
- Business cards with your contact details, including email address
- Good typing, spelling and grammar skills
- Administration skills

Although there are no formal prerequisites for becoming a virtual assistant, you need to learn the ropes before you jump in feet-first.

There is also some excellent virtual assistant software available that helps you to run your empire at home:

- **Hubstaff** is a way for your clients to monitor what you do during the day. The program takes a screenshot of your computer every ten minutes or so – and the client has access to this screenshot. This is a particularly good resource for you if you have employees under you, so you can monitor their work. It is also a great project management tool and a place you can store all your files and discussions regarding a client.

- **Dropbox** is a cloud-based file-sharing tool that is free to use, but you can scale up the storage with a paid account if you need it.

- **Google Calendar** is brilliant – if you haven't started using it already for your personal life, you should! It's a great way to set up appointments, remember deadlines and share the details for upcoming events with others.

- **LastPass** is a password management program that has saved me time and headaches! You know how you need to remember a squillion passwords for everything in your everyday life these days? Well, with LastPass I only need one really strong password, and it remembers the rest of them for me!

While you're setting yourself up, it's a good idea to join various LinkedIn and Facebook groups so you can meet other virtual assistants and trade information. Here are a few:

- Virtual Assistants Australia
- Virtual Assistant Network (Australia)

- VA Institute of Australia
- VA Directory

How to market yourself as a virtual assistant

Once you've done some research and set yourself up, it's time to start earning some money. And to do that, you need to market your business and get the word out there that you're looking for work. I recommend the following basic marketing strategies such as:

- Start your own Facebook page, detailing your location and services offered.
- Go to local business meetings and events to tell people about what you do.
- Have happy customers leave reviews.
- Put together a media kit (a pack that shows all the tasks you can do for your clients, along with your rates) – I put mine together in Canva (which is free).

In your media kit, you want to accentuate the aspects you're good at, and leave out the things you don't know. If there is demand for a service about which you have limited knowledge, this is where you should look at upskilling. On the other hand, remember that not all virtual assistants do all jobs; in fact, if you specialise in a particular area, you could demand more money for your services.

Think of a media kit much like a résumé. Try to keep it to a single page if you can. You should include:

- Typing speed and accuracy – rate per word or per hour
- Computer programs that you are competent in
- Other skills you have, such as data entry or social media management
- Contact details, including your email address and mobile number

On the important question of rates, you need to take all your costs into account, your experience, and what other virtual assistants in your location and area of expertise are charging. You may want to consider charging for a whole job, rather than an hourly rate.

Start your own business in the fashion industry

If you have an interest in the fashion industry and have a good eye for designing fashion, can predict the latest fashions or can sew, consider starting your own fashion boutique or look for a niche in the fashion industry.

In the past, the fashion industry was notoriously hard to break into and it is still very competitive. But now there are online platforms such as Etsy or Madeit that have a ready-made audience of people looking for handmade items that are not mass-produced. Best of all, many of these customers are willing to pay big dollars for quality items.

The key to doing well in the fashion industry (like all industries) is finding your little niche in the market. Some of the trending fashion niches include:

Slow fashion	Upcycled fashion	Women's workwear
High-end shoes	Clubbing wear	Over 40s fashion
Handmade fashion for kids	Maternity wedding gowns	Maternity shoot gowns
Eco and ethical fashion	Sewing tutorials	Replica vintage fashion
Latex lingerie	Knitting tutorials	Design your own fabrics
Eco swimwear made from recycled plastics	Bamboo designer undies	

There are two ways to start your own fashion boutique: purchasing items from a clothing manufacturer or distributor to resell at a profit, or creating items by hand from scratch. Let's go through both.

Find stock to resell

Not everyone can sew or has the patience and knowledge to design a garment. But all is not lost. You can source garments from a clothing manufacturer.

The most common way to start a fashion line is to buy items from a clothing manufacturer's website (generally in bulk), then resell those items for a profit.

To do this you need to have an eye for great designs that you think will sell well – and be able to do that up to 12 months in advance, trying to predict what will be popular. Most clothing boutiques do it this way. If you find a brand of clothing that you really like in a current boutique, you can look up the label to find the manufacturer and approach them for a wholesale price per item. The only problem with this method is that you need quite a bit of money up-front to purchase the clothing in a range of sizes. A manufacturer's 'minimum order quantity' is usually the three words of doom for a newbie wanting to get their foot in the door.

It takes time (and money) to build a relationship with a manufacturer to get the clothing at a decent discounted price to make the venture worthwhile, at least locally. You can usually find cheaper prices overseas. If you are looking at importing you need to consider the following:

- Quality of the garments (always get a sample)
- Import duties and taxes
- Conditions and possible exploitation of workers located in developing countries

For a list of clothing manufacturers both in Australia and overseas, check out this link: www.stayathomemum.com.au/bodyand soul/fashion/free-list-of-clothing-manufacturers-both-australian-and-overseas/

Once you have stock, you can start a simple website (see section 8.3 for how to do that), including great photos of your product, ideally on models. Then like any business you will need to market your store to get sales (see Chapter 9). And there you go – you have started your own fashion business!

Create your own garments

If you are a gun on the sewing machine and your work is excellent quality, you can make your own garments to sell. The best thing about this is that your garments will be far more unique than anything you buy from a manufacturer in bulk. Remember that many high-end fashion designers are self-taught and started at home behind their sewing machine.

Start small with just a few quality pieces. This way you don't have a huge outlay to begin with and you can test the market to see what sells and what doesn't. You can even offer custom items if you're creating individual pieces rather than trying to sell a large quantity of the same item.

As you get word out there and some happy customers, you can build up demand and build your brand from there. You can even start creating your own patterns and fabrics to stand out from the crowd even more. Making money from your own creations will feel amazing!

Start a subscription box business

Putting together a curated selection of goods is a fabulous way to start your own business, so let's look at how to get started. Boxes can be monthly, every two or three months or one-offs, and they make fantastic gifts, which is why subscritpion boxes have really taken off. In this section, we'll look at where to find products to stock in your subscription box, how to market them, and how you might go about selling them.

To make your box appealing to your demographic, ensure it's good value for money, that it's nicely packed and presented, and that you keep the contents fresh and surprising. If you can also provide great customer service, you will have customers coming back again and again!

You name it and there's a box available for it. But some boxes are a lot more popular than others. The most popular boxes I've seen are in the following categories:

- Make-up and beauty
- Health and fitness, including period items or weight-loss
- Pets
- Books
- Fashion

- Food lovers
- Ethically sourced items
- Boxes aimed specifically at men
- Parenting, baby and children
- Adults only
- Specific interests and hobbies, such as sewing and craft
- Tea and coffee

Sourcing products to put in your subscription box

Where to source products for your subscription box depends, of course, on what you're looking for. But let's look at some great ideas to get you started. Remember though, before ordering large quantities, try a sample first to make sure the product is exactly what you're looking for.

If you have a specific brand or product in mind, email the producer directly to see if they offer a wholesale price on bulk buys to make your endeavour worthwhile and profitable. See if you can find an actual name to address your email to (LinkedIn helps with this) and send something along these lines:

> *I have started a new subscription box business and plan to sell it to [insert your target customer). I'm interested in purchasing [your desired quantity] units of your product [insert product name here] on a regular basis, and am wondering what wholesale price you may be able to offer me.*
>
> *I'm hoping to get my first lot of boxes out in [insert time frame] – can you work within this timeframe? Looking forward to helping your products reach a new audience.*

Packaging your subscription box

Packaging is a huge consideration. Think about what will protect the products from damage in transit. How you can make it look pretty, but also safe from being ruined if something should leak?

As well as the practicalities of shipping, your packaging is a reflection of your brand. So having a plastic container for an eco-friendly box just won't look right. Think about the products you are selling and how you would like them to be viewed. Imagine it is you receiving the box for the first time. How does it look? What colour is it? Is it a cardboard box? Is it wrapped in paper, tied with ribbon or does it have a sticker on the front? The possibilities are endless. Look at the competition for inspiration and see how you can make it your own if you want yours to stand out from the crowd.

Branding your subscription box business

The most exciting part of starting a new business is to choose your branding. Personally, I think you should always go with what you like rather than just following what everyone else is doing. If you adore yellow, make your logo yellow. Choose an image you love to become part of your brand – because your brand reflects you!

Of course, there are loads of professionals out there who can design your branding. But I always suggest starting small and building from there rather than spending a lot of extra money up front. To start, choose an online photo-editing website to make up something simple (they are free). I like PicMonkey and Canva.

Pricing your subscription box

Start a spreadsheet listing how much every item costs (including postage) and how much your packaging is to determine your costs, and add a mark-up to make a profit. Profit margins on subscription boxes should be between 25 and 30%. Compare this with other niche product boxes that are similar to yours and check out their price points.

Decide whether postage is to be a separate cost to the buyer or if you'll build it in. Keep in mind that the lighter your subscription box, the cheaper it will be to post – and postage cost is a consideration that people make when purchasing. Once you have a finished box, pop down to your local post office to check how much it would be to mail your box both in Australia and overseas.

Consider whether your box will be a one-off box, a monthly box or a gift box. You might consider offering discounts to people who buy or subscibe to two or more boxes as an incentive.

Selling your subscription box

Okay, so you've organised your subscription box – now, you need to find a platform on which to sell it. You can set up your own website to sell the boxes, but keep in mind that you'll need a payment system and a way to manage all the shipping yourself. It's often easier to outsource all of these; for example, by looking into these websites who can sell your boxes for a commission:

- CrateJoy
- Subbly
- Etsy

Marketing your subscription box business

It's time to let the world know about your subscription box and entice people to buy it! There are multiple ways in which you can market your business, including social media, where you can show pictures of your product and tell your customers why they will love it.

Another way is to persuade influencers try your box and review it on their blog or in a video, or have your box listed on one of the many subscription box lists going around.

Word of mouth is the most powerful way to get the message out about your subscription box. So tell your friends and family, and have them tell their friends and families. Make your social media images gorgeous and appealing. Have good customer service – and you could be onto a winner.

Other business ideas

The next section provides potential business ideas that might be perfect for you, depending on your skills and interests. For even more ideas, check out the tables in the Appendix.

Gourmet bread

If you love making bread at home, and have access to a commercial kitchen (this is essential if you're going to sell it), why not make your famous sourdough and sell your loaves to local cafes, delis and specialty food stores? If you can make a really lovely gluten-free bread or something really artisanal, you can charge more for your product.

Look for a commercial kitchen space you can rent or fitout your own kitchen to meet the necessary health and safety standards for your state or territory. Check with your local council for any permits required for your local area. You charge prices on a 'per loaf' basis, depending on how fancy the bread is. You can start selling your bread at local markets and build up from there (see Chapter 5 for more on markets).

Cake baking and decorating

If your family and friends are always begging you to make that delectable cake with amazing icing for their special occasions, why not look at using your skills to make cakes for your business? Whether it's cupcakes for a school birthday, or wedding cakes and everything in between, you can create a dedicated Facebook page or Instagram account to showcase your work and start charging for your services. A good cake decorator is always in demand.

You can decorate cupcakes for birthday parties, do anniversary cakes, wedding cakes – or any other occasion you can think of. There are loads of YouTube and Facebook tutorials around for inspiration and to help you learn the required skills, along with short courses (in-person or online).

Ensure that the food is made in a commercial kitchen or one that meets the necessary health and safety standards for your state or territory, and check with your local council about any permits you might need. A basic but stunningly decorated wedding cake can go for as much as $300, while for a fairly simple birthday cake you might be looking at the $80 mark. The level of skill and complexity of design will increase the cost of the cake.

Cake-decorating classes

Cake decorating is always a popular skill with much interest for mums. You can hold classes in a commercial kitchen, or you can even do lessons online, which opens your courses up to people all around the world.

Here are some cake decorating niches that might drum up more interest than a generic cake-decorating class:

- Naughty cakes
- Wedding cakes
- Kids' party cakes
- Naked cakes

You can easily charge from $100 per person for a two-hour class, but remember that this must include the costs for renting the space, advertising and ingredients. For online classes you would charge significantly less because you don't have those overheads – but you can offer the course to a lot more people at once too.

Home cookery

If you're a strong cook and don't mind spending time in the kitchen, you're set to offer your services for busy families who don't have time to cook a delicious dinner at night. You might provide pre-prepared foods or even cook at your client's house and serve dinner straight to the table! You can expect to earn from $10 per serving.

Ever heard of HelloFresh, Marley Spoon or Dinnerly? You could be the next big thing with your own meal prep kit for busy people. If you want to go big, think of creating a website so your customers can pick and choose their own meals and dietary choices.

Always check with your local council as to food preparation requirements, such as whether you need to use a commercial kitchen, whether you need any licences and what food labelling requirements you need to meet.

Fitness food

Super-fit people are very particular about what they eat. Many choose food that is high in protein, low in carbs and meets all of their dietary requirements. This can take a lot of time and effort to put together. If you're interested in nutrients and measuring macros, starting a fitness food preparation business might be for you! Put together meal plans or fully prepared meals that you can deliver straight to your customers.

Different niches within this business could include ketogenic, vegan, high protein or macrobiotic.

To really make your business outstanding, have your plans and meals reviewed by a dietitian. You can expect to charge from $10 per meal. Always check with your local council as to food preparation requirements, such as whether you need to use a commercial kitchen, whether you need any licences and what food labelling requirements you need to meet.

Tea blends

If you have a good palate for flavoured teas, why not look at creating your very own blend of tea and selling it for a profit? For under $100 you could purchase a range of teas to blend, and you can keep the packaging attractive but simple. I've even seen tea blends sold in super adorable test tube containers. Make sure you check out any laws around importing teas, food safety and handling, and labelling requirements – some teas are not good for people on certain medications or with certain conditions, so health warnings might be essential.

You could sell your new tea blend at a local market, on Etsy or just start up your very own Facebook page. Ask influencers to try your tea.

These are really popular ideas for wedding favours too.

You can purchase tea from reputable sellers (you must have top quality!) such as:

- T2 Tea is based in Australia and offers specialty teas and tools.
- Kusmi Tea is a luxury tea supplier based in Paris.
  You can pick up clear test tubes with stoppers from:
- InTheClear on Etsy sells a multitude of tubes at reasonable prices.
- ElvesNFairies on Etsy sells plastic test tubes with metal screw tops.

Wrap them in bubble-wrap to post in a box with a little twine tie and label – and you are set!

Hair or beauty products

Organic and vegan make-up and skincare products are in high demand. If you have a recipe for a magical clay mask or a moisturising cream that your friends love, consider making small batches and selling it to others who will appreciate your handmade products. Many small operators making their own beauty products start out selling their range on Etsy.

Since safety and labelling requirements for cosmetics can be quite tricky, you'll need to learn more about it before starting your business. Find out more from the Australian Competition and Consumer Commission (ACCC).

Make-up artist

If you have a knack for helping people look incredible with your make-up skills, or if you have a bit of a thing for stage make-up, consider advertising your services for hire in the make-up industry. Whether you specialise in a classic style for spring racing, something sinister for Halloween, a full bridal look, or any make-up artistry challenge that's put to you, take loads of pictures of your work (with your models' consent) and post them on your business Facebook page and Instagram. To get a bit of practice under your belt, you might approach local theatre or dancing groups to do their make-up for performances.

As well as posting your work on social media, there is now Flayr, an app where you can advertise your services in your local area and get bookings directly – just like an Airbnb but for hair and make-up. You can set your own pricing for all sorts of services, depending on what you're good at.

You can expect to earn from $80 for a basic make-up look to as much as $300 for wedding make-up. If you also include hair services, you can easily double that.

What you will need to start:

- A good quality make-up kit
- A smartphone
- Ring light to take good quality photographs of your work

You can put notices in high-school newsletters for end-of-school formals, local newspapers for brides, and get to know hairdressers who will recommend your work (perhaps offering them a commission for referring your work, and similarly you can send make-up clients to them).

Personalisation

People love things with their own names on them. I know many mums who get a real kick out of decking their kids' rooms out with items that have their names all over them. The beauty of this type of business is that you can pretty much personalise anything! This is just the tip of the iceberg:

- Custom wooden name plaques
- Dolls and teddies with names embroidered on them
- Books and stationery
- T-shirts
- Jewellery boxes
- Bracelets and other fashion accessories
- Handbags and schoolbags

You can choose whether to make a niche of kids', men's or women's items, or cover the whole family and focus on a particular style of personalisation, such as embroidery, etching, monogramming or screenprinting. Your mode of personalisation will also help to guide your price point. The options are endless.

Jewellery

Jewellery never goes out of style, so why not consider starting your own small business selling unique jewellery? Even if you don't have the artistry or training to make your own, you can market wholesale jewellery. See the list on page 166.

To market your business, promote pieces on Facebook and Instagram, hold local jewellery parties or rent a stall at a local market (see Chapter 5 for more about markets).

Sell images to stock image websites

You don't need to be a professional photographer to make money selling your photographs. Many stock image sites, such as iStock, Shutterstock and Bigstock, are always looking for day-to-day photographs of people doing 'normal people things'. All you do is upload your photos and assign appropriate keywords so people searching for images will find them, and then you'll start making money as people pay to use the photos in their work.

Check the terms and conditions carefully to see what you will get paid and whether or not you retain the copyright of the image. You can expect to be paid from $2.50 per download per image. If your image becomes really popular, you could earn thousands of dollars from a single image.

Here are some more sites to check out (but there are hundreds out there):
- Alamy
- Stockify
- Fotolia
- Crestock
- 123RF
- Corbis
- Dreamstime
- Getty Images

Flat-lay photography

If you have a good camera and a discerning eye for colours and style, consider becoming a flat-lay photographer! Offer your services to businesses that need pretty photographs of their stock for social media. Grab unique backdrops from your local flooring or fabric centre (see if you can buy off-cuts in many different colours and styles).

Photograph the items from overhead, lighting them perfectly and snap – with just a little post-processing you have a beautiful flat-lay image. Images can be styled and sold from $100 plus. You could even run a course on how to do flat-lay photography!

If you love the idea but your photography skills aren't up to scratch, you might find a designer or photographer online and pay them an hourly rate for doing all the styling and photographs themselves. You then become the manager and can sell multiple photographs to multiple buyers – and even list those photographs for sale on various stock photography sites.

Advertise via Instagram by showing clients your skills and tagging them in the images or on local business Facebook groups.

Design apps

If you have a great idea for a new app, and are willing to follow through to get it made and marketed to your customers, it can prove very lucrative. You will need to outline how your app will work, the images that you want and the general functionality it should have. Then you can provide that to an app developer who can make your dream app a reality.

The potential cost of having your app idea developed could be anywhere between $5000 and $350,000 depending on quality and functionality, so this is not for the faint-hearted!

Start a YouTube channel

Creating a YouTube channel is easier than it's ever been nowadays, but the trick is in maintaining the channel, posting new material regularly, and getting enough subscribers to create income out of it. Watch lots of YouTube videos across a wide range of topics, and do some research about how to monetise your channel. If you can get a minimum of 4000 views on Youtube per month, you can usually start finding sponsorship and product reviewing opportunities! You'll need wit, charm and lots of fresh ideas. Once you're established, you can expect to make from $200 per 60-second video.

Create educational videos

Do you have a special interest or talent to share with the world? Educational videos are fun to make and can help you generate income. Your video should be brief, easy to understand, entertaining and backed by facts. Just like blogging, income-generating opportunities are generally in the form of advertising and/or affiliate marketing. Make sure to research for trendy topics to keep your video ideas fresh.

Family history researcher

Many people are interested in the genealogy of their family, but simply don't have the time or patience to do it, so why not put your research skills to work and become a family history researcher for other people! There are amazing websites around now that help you trace your family tree back as far as it will go. They even have access to birth certificates, wedding certificates and details of where your ancestors lived.

Approach your local family history society to get a bit of know-how under your belt, then advertise locally. Sign up to a genealogy website so that you have access to records. Here are some sites to look at, though keep in mind that you'll have to pay for a subscription:

- Ancestry
- Findmypast
- FamilySearch
- MyHeritage
  You can expect to earn from $20 per hour.

Fact checker

Media organisations and authors who are writing historical or period books often need the assistance of fact checkers to make sure they are being as accurate as possible with what they are writing. Contrary to what some may believe, not everything is just a Google search away – checkers are needed in many contexts to verify facts and ensure a publication is free of gaps or misinterpreted information.

If you love delving deep into research and are a stickler for detail, this could be the perfect gig for you!

Résumé writing

If you are diligent with spelling and grammar and know how to talk someone up, there's great demand for services around professional résumé writing and cover letters. Not everyone knows how to put together a professional-looking résumé, but everyone knows how important it is to get them right. Advertise your services on local Facebook pages and noticeboards.

There are thousands of beautiful résumé templates online that are free to access, to give you a few ideas to start yours from. You can expect to be paid from $300 per résumé and cover letter. You can also sell your résumé template on sites such as Etsy as a downloadable, which we covered in Chapter 4.

Packing services

What you're selling here is your labour and time – but more importantly, a quick and hassle-free experience for customers who are moving and have no time to pack everything themselves. This is perfect for people who have great organisational skills and enough manpower on call to help out with the heavy lifting. To thrive in this kind of business, you'll need to connect with real estate people who can recommend you to get the job done. You'll also need transportation, manpower, boxes, containers and other packing materials.

Wedding favours

If you are someone who loves to do craft, then you could be well suited to creating a wedding bomboniere (wedding favours or keepsakes) business.

What's great about this is you can start small and build from there. Your first customers can be your close family and friends, and then word-of-mouth can really take over. Make sure to take photos of your creations and upload them to your social media to gain wider exposure.

Look at what others are doing and find a way to put your own spin on your favours to stand out from the crowd. You can appeal to bigger and more profitable weddings by offering discounts for large orders.

For the materials you'll need, here are some sources for wholesale wedding favours:

- My Wedding Favors
- SuperBuys Warehouse
- AliExpress

Non-floral wedding bouquets

These days, unique wedding bouquets can be made from everything from latex to newspaper! There aren't many options around for non-floral wedding bouquets, so designing and selling them is a really great idea for people looking for something unique that won't wilt on the big day. Create some prototypes and post images of them online, which will also encourage enquiries for different designs or materials!

As well as selling through social media, you can sell your bouquets on eBay, Etsy and in local florist shops.

Gift baskets

If you're into creating gift baskets for your family and friends, then consider turning this into a small business. Gift baskets are great because they can be customised according to what the receiver likes (for example, luxury food, wine, toys – you name it) and adjusted to whatever budget. You'll need to have creative and entrepreneurial skills as well as basic marketing ability.

Professional pet sitter

With more and more people adopting fur babies that they can't bear to put in a kennel when they go away, hiring a pet sitter who will visit your pet each day to feed them, check their environment, walk them if needed and provide care and affection is becoming a more popular option. You will need to have good transport, know how to take care of animals and be trustworthy. A pet-sitting business is a low-cost business start-up that usually runs on word of mouth, but keep in mind that you will require public liability insurance.

Holiday decorator

I adore Christmas, but don't particularly like putting up the Christmas decorations – or taking them down, for that matter! If you relish doing this kind of job, and can put together the perfect Christmas tree, why not capitalise on this leading up to the holidays? And it isn't just households that put up Christmas decorations – you can approach local commercial businesses and shopping centres too. You can also offer a take-down service for after Christmas.

Of course, this kind of work isn't just limited to Christmas. Other ideas include:

- Kids' birthday party decorating
- Staging homes for sale (house stylist)
- Commercial functions such as balls or dances
- Wedding styling

Some clients might even get you to purchase the decorations for the job. Grab them wholesale from The Christmas Warehouse.

Create art for homewares

Are you into calligraphy or someone who loves to draw? Designing your own line of art prints and then uploading them for use on products could be a great business idea for you. A number of websites allow anyone to choose your design and have it printed on an item of their choice – and you get commission on the sale. Items with printed artwork include:

- Framed or mounted prints
- Throw pillows
- Doona covers
- Crockery
- Phone cases

Here are some sites where you can upload your artwork for use on products:

- Society6
- Designhill

- Etsy
- Threadless
- Creative Market
- Art Web
- Spreadshop
- Zazzle
- Redbubble

Design and sell funny T-shirts

Create funny designs and have them printed on T-shirts for your very own T-shirt line. You can use Facebook, Instagram or a dedicated website to sell your clothes online. The great thing about selling T-shirts is that you can organise to have them dropshipped really easily; for example, by using Shopify (more on this in Chapter 8).

See page 161 for a list of on-demand T-shirt suppliers, and for inspiration, check out US-based company T-Shirt Hell – their designs are truly hysterical!

Create your own line of activewear

Activewear is big business and there's increasing crossover between sporty and stylish. If you have a bit of design sense, you can now create your very own range of activewear, in any colour, style or shape you wish. There are loads of manufacturers out there that will make your designs to spec without requiring huge orders.

For an inspiring example of someone who has done it well, check out Sunday Morning Active, an Etsy store that sells activewear inspired by the outfits worn by Disney princesses! They are unique and gorgeous.

A few places you can get your activewear manufactured:
- Slyletica
- Hingto
- DK Active
- Ethical Clothing Australia

Buy and sell vintage clothing

Do you get excited when you score amazing pieces of vintage clothing at the op shop? If you've got a great eye for this, why not consider it as a business? There is a growing demand for vintage clothing as many people want sustainable clothing, as well as something that's truly unique and distinct from today's fast fashion. Do your research, look around at what is in demand, and sell your vintage finds at a profit.

If you don't want to set up your own website for vintage clothing, there are specialised platforms catering to just this, including:

- thredUP
- Poshmark
- Tradesy
- Refashioner
- Depop
- Yordrobe
- SWOP
- The Vault

Ensure you use great lighting to take detailed photographs of your clothing, use a model if you can, and ensure you give a full report of the branding, measurements and any flaws.

Children's party entertainer

Do you love making people laugh and are you good with kids? If you have passion for entertainment and performing, then that's a great combination for someone to start a kids' party entertainment business. With this business, you are in charge of the fun at a kid's party. You can do magic, clowning, juggling, storytelling, puppets, face-painting and the like.

You'll need to organise transportation, music, party props, face paint and other necessary equipment.

You can advertise your services on:

- CrowdPleaser
- Entertainers Factory
- Enhance Entertainment

- Fly By Fun
- Kiddly-Winks
- Airtasker, Gumtree, etc.

Small business marketing

You don't need a marketing degree to do some small-scale work for local businesses in your area. If you have loads of contacts, nifty ideas for promoting a business, and loads of get up and go, you're made to become a small business marketer.

Approach small businesses with your rates and a business card. Look at places like pubs, small corner shops, bowling alleys or skating rinks. Think about what is the best way to promote their business and put together a one-page marketing plan on how you would go about it to attract clients.

Sell products on consignment

If you have the time and patience to list products online for sale, you could consider selling goods on consignment. This means that you essentially act as a sales agent on someone else's behalf – you sell the products for them and get a percentage for each sale. You can sell via your Facebook page or store, or on sites such as eBay or Gumtree. One great thing about this business model is that you have the right to return goods that don't get sold.

Good products to sell on consignment include:

- Vehicles
- Vintage clothing and handbags
- Jewellery

Swimming instructor

Becoming a private swimming instructor can be a great gig, especially in the summer months. To start your swimming instructor business, you'll need professional certification and insurance according to your state's requirements, and ideally experience as a swimming coach.

Having your own swimming pool would be more convenient because if you need to use a public swimming pool, you'll usually pay a higher rate than just swimming entry, as you're competing with their contracted instructors. You will also need permission from the pool contractors.

Buy and flip websites

Buying websites and flipping (selling for a profit) them can be a great way to generate income. It is basically about buying a website that is not performing well or at all, improving it so that it starts to perform consistently, and then selling it for a profit. You'll need knowledge of web design and an understanding of the industry to be successful but you can learn as you go. Look at website sellers such as Flippa.com.

Home organiser

If your filing cabinet is a work of art and you're often tempted to sort out other people's pantries or wardrobes, consider becoming a home organiser. Word of mouth is the key here, plus Instagramming amazing before and after photos your work. You could also advertise on local job boards, hand out flyers to the local daycare centres and schools, and talk to other mums who are too busy to do the job themselves!

Experienced home organisers can command thousands of dollars for a project, especially if they're dealing with years' worth of clutter. But if you are just starting out, you'll need to price your services accordingly until you build your reputation.

Garage sale organiser

A lot of people are interested in holding garage sales, but can't have one because they don't have a good venue to do so. If you have a space that's good for holding garage sales and convenient for displaying preloved stuff, that's a great start as you can rent this out for a flat fee per sale, and then charge for extra services. If you don't have such a space and instead want to be a garage sale organiser in someone's else's space, then you would be charging clients to manage everything for their event at their home, including setting up the space and goods for sale, marketing the event and making sure the entire thing runs smoothly.

One of your tasks will be helping the seller price their goods, so a good understanding of the market is essential.

Party or event planning

For a party or event planning business, you need to be extremely organised, detail-oriented and resourceful, as well as a people person. The ideal party planner relishes the opportunity to bring joy into people's lives through well organised events. To be successful, you will need contacts in food and venues, and possess good creative problem solving skills for when issues crop up during events.

Party and event planners organise:

- Birthday parties, especially significant birthdays
- Weddings
- Hens' and bucks' nights
- High teas

The real money, however, is in organising business and corporate events, which requires much bigger scale planning.

Although there are no formal qualifications required to be a party planner, you can do a degree in event management, which will give you an edge in the industry.

A word on weddings

Being a wedding organiser is no easy job as the expectations are sky-high, but if you have a passion for organising and the skills to pull it off, this can be a lucrative gig, as anything associated with weddings can command big bucks.

If you're new to the industry, you need to do lots of homework, including familiarising yourself with the latest trends in the wedding industry, so hit up magazines, blogs and wedding expos if you want to learn the lingo. Basically, being a wedding organiser means making sure the happy couple remain stress-free and the day runs smoothly.

Marriage celebrant

Working as a marriage celebrant can be a flexible, enjoyable and rewarding way to make money. The job involves preparing all the legal documents required when a couple plans to marry, ensuring that you cover all the legal responsibilities when it comes to the service, discussing the vows and assisting with preparing the wedding and officiating at the service.

You will be required to have a Certificate IV in Celebrancy that is offered by TAFE or other registered training providers. You will also need to dress impeccably for the service, be super organised and have a confident manner.

Being a celebrant involves a yearly fee of $240 (correct at time of print) and a one-off initial application fee of $600. This can sometimes be waived if you live in a very remote area or if no other marriage celebrants live in your area, though you still have to pay a small fee.

You can find work through word of mouth, or have a dedicated Facebook page. Consider including reviews from your previous clients or even pretty pictures from their weddings if they're happy to allow it.

Massage therapist

Got a spare room, strong hands and an interest in human anatomy? Why not get your qualifications in massage therapy? You will need a nice quiet private room, a good sturdy professional massage table, a smart phone and perhaps a scheduling app for taking bookings. Some therapists also offer a mobile service where they take their table to the client's home.

Qualifications required include a Certificate IV in Massage Therapy, and you can do further study by completing a Diploma of Remedial Massage.

Mobile spray tanner

If you can give yourself an awesome tan at home, why not look at starting a mobile spray-tanning business? You don't need any qualifications besides being able to travel to customers' homes to give them a beautiful tan on demand.

In terms of required equipment, a small spray tan kit plus some good-quality tan solution is sufficient to start out. A tanning tent is handy too, to ensure the spray doesn't get all over the client's bathroom, but you can always adapt a shower curtain. A semi-professional spray tanning gun retails for about $300.

You should be able to charge from $50 for offering clients a fantastic tan in the privacy of their own home.

Life coach

If you are known as a super positive person who achieves everything you set out to, life coaching could be a wonderful business option for you. Life coaches help others to set goals personally, professionally and financially, and then help their clients work towards those goals and stay accountable. Although there are no designated educational requirements to become a life coach, if you have some training in psychology or education, or have a background in the military or personal training, this could be a huge plus.

Life coaches can command as much as $300 per hour, although when starting out I would recommend a rate more around the $50 per hour mark until you get some runs on the board.

Garden designer

Many people can't afford a landscape architect – and the role does often involve years of education and training. But if you have a green thumb and a knack for creating beautiful gardens, consider becoming a freelance garden designer. Besides the actual design, if you can do some of the actual gardening work – or even supply the plants – you can make even more money.

It would be an advantage to have a background in horticulture or working for a nursery, and a strong knowledge of which plants will work in different environments.

For a simple garden design, you can charge as much as $300. If you are also doing the work, you can charge an hourly rate of $25–35.

Travel consultant

With many people time poor or not computer savvy, there is a great opportunity to assist in putting holidays together into packages including transportation, accommodation and any other activities. There are no formal qualifications to become a travel consultant, though most people learn on the job at a travel agency before venturing out on their own. A travel consultant needs to be super organised and unflappable, a good listener to help identify a client's dream holiday and the ability and contacts to find the best and cheapest deals to make the client's travel itinerary seamless.

Car detailer

If you have room in a garage or shed with access to water and electricity and a good vacuum, a car detailing business could keep you extremely busy! You will require a manual licence, public liability insurance and an impeccable driving history.

If you offer environmentally friendly products for use on vehicles, you can generally charge more. Offering a pick-up and drop-off service will ensure you get even more customers.

Advertise your services on Facebook and get your customers to promote you via word of mouth. You can charge up to $200 for a large vehicle to be detailed inside and out.

House cleaner

If you have a reliable car, some basic cleaning products and physical stamina, house cleaning is one of the easiest businesses to start. Advertise your services on noticeboards, local Facebook pages and by word of mouth (tell your local hairdresser) – and get cleaning.

Happy clients are usually willing to pay $30 per hour. You could charge more if you offer environmentally friendly products, which will also help you stand out from the crowd.

Start a local website

Are you someone who always has your ear to the ground and knows what's going on in your community? You could start a website about all the things that are happening, local stories, activities for kids, new businesses and functions, ways to keep the community involved, events happening in your area, or even keep people up to date during a disaster or pandemic. While this won't make you money to begin with, once it's up and running and attracting a decent audience, you can begin charging advertising space on a dedicated website.

Starting a website doesn't have to be expensive – there are plenty of cheap or even free website platforms out there if you have an eye for detail and style. Even a directory website is a great way to start building traffic by offering free listings until you build up a following.

You will need to build up your audience first, but have an advertising page listing all the services you offer. You can also include sponsored stories, website banners or promotion of an event.

The more readership you have, the more you can charge for advertising. Don't expect to make money in the beginning, but if you have the patience to build build build, it can be very lucrative in the long run.

Recipe creator and photographer

Foodies who can develop unique recipes and photograph them beautifully can sell them to recipe blogs for publishing. You can create your own recipes, or you can take requests. Not only can you sell your recipes but you could branch out into creating your own cookbook, website or cooking school – there are so many options.

Where to get work as a recipe creator:
- Approach food companies.
- Enter recipe-making contests for exposure.
- Approach food magazines to sell your recipes.
- Advertise your recipes for sale on foodie Facebook Groups.
- Publish an electronic cookbook.
- Start a food blog.
- Pitch your recipes to food bloggers.

A good recipe with beautiful images can command $100 or more, depending on how complicated and unique the recipe is.

Sewing and alterations

Sewing is really becoming an art that fewer people are proficient in, so if you have learned this valuable skill, you can use it to make money. If your skills are quite basic, you can start by offering very simple alterations such as adding buttons or fixing hems, then as your skills increase, you can progress to more advanced clothing alterations and eventually custom work.

Advertise your services on a dedicated Facebook page, or approach your local sewing centre or fabric shop to keep your details on file for people who enquire about such services.

Gutter and solar panel cleaner

Cleaning out dirt and leaf debris from house gutters isn't a glamorous job; however, it is a necessary one. If you don't mind climbing up ladders and getting your hands dirty, you can make a pretty good living.

Just like a gutter cleaner, solar panel cleaning is a job that not many homeowners want to do as it involves getting up on a roof. But where people don't want to do something, there lies an opportunity for others to make money.

You will need a long ladder, a ute or similar, a high-pressure cleaner, protective clothing and good public liability insurance. You can find work by advertising in local newspapers and Facebook groups, or drop your flyers with local property managers and real estate agents – especially for rentals where property owners can claim the cost on tax.

You can charge from $200 per standard single-storey house for gutter cleaning, and it goes up from there for larger houses or apartment buildings with second storeys. Check out what the competition is charging.

Oven cleaner

This is another job around the house that many people hate doing, so if you're the rare breed who finds great satisfaction in restoring a grotty oven to sparkling cleanliness, you can make money doing just that, either as your dedicated line of work or as a feature of your wider cleaning business. You will need a reliable vehicle, cleaning products and a good set of gloves.

Advertise your services to local cleaning companies, property managers (this is a great end-of-lease service) and on local Facebook groups. You can expect to charge from $100 per oven clean.

Small business fulfilment service

If you have a roomy garage or secure shed with plenty of space, you could be the intermediary between small businesses and their customers by offering a fulfilment service. Many small businesses want to outsource the actual postage and handling of their products so that they can focus on building the business instead of being overwhelmed with the process of packaging. You would stock all of a small business's products at your location, and when a sale comes through, you post the item directly to the customer.

If you have the room to store the products (ideally enough to store more than one client's products) and live close enough to a postal centre to deliver all the parcels daily, this could be the business for you. You can negotiate how much per parcel or per month you charge with each client.

Customer service representative

Customer service assistants are the face (or voice) of a company and you can offer your services to established businesses who want to outsource this. In this instance, you are the go-to person responsible for helping customers with any questions or concerns they may have. Yes, it might mean that you cop a blast or two from unhappy customers, so having a cheery disposition and a thick skin are essential – remember, they are not mad at *you,* just the situation they are in.

This style of job is now more accessible for stay-at-home mums as businesses are sending their clients through phone lines or email portals to deal with enquiries and complaints. You will need to be committed to learning everything you can about the business you are representing, as well as the policies they have for client management.

Flatpack builder

Are you a sucker for a great Ikea flatpack buildfest? You can turn this passion into a thriving business, fulfilling a need for people who loathe this pastime – you just may save a marriage or two in the process! You can offer your service based on the size or complexity of the project. You may head out to the client to build on site, or if you want to stay at home, you can choose whether to include delivery of the completed furniture if you have the vehicle for it – for an extra fee, of course.

Trivia question creator

Trivia nights are a great way for non-profit organisations and schools to make extra income. And if you have a knack for putting together questions and answers, there could be an opportunity for you to make money too.

Putting together different styles of questions and quizzes for different audiences and on different themes is a talent – and you can sell whole trivia night sets to not only non-profits but companies all over the world. As well as preparing questions, you could offer to run the trivia nights as well.

Hot tip: Act when you see a need! A good friend of mine was up on her roof cleaning solar panels one day, when her elderly neighbour asked her to do her solar panels too. One neighbour turned into a whole street, one street became a neighbourhood, and now my friend employs five people to wash solar panels! Think of the things that you need done around the house, and what your neighbours might need doing; find that niche, and start a business doing just that.

Conclusion

In this chapter, you've considered some of the typical attributes that successful entrepreneurs possess. You've also wrestled with whether you already have an idea for a perfect business. You've brainstormed ideas based on what you're good at, what inspires you, and what you can't abide. Can you bring passion to your drive to start a business? Now you've got some ideas, I'll show you how to get started.

Chapter 7

Time for lift off!

Starting and running a successful business requires a lot of hard work, effort and time. Most people end up failing because of lack of determination, patience and planning. Many throw in the towel in the initial phases of starting a business, overwhelmed by common setbacks, but if your venture survives, the rewards are well worth all the challenges you will face on the journey to success – and there will always be challenges! In this chapter, I'll step you through a comprehensive guide on how to set up a brand-new business.

7.1 Build your idea

All the successful businesses out there started with an idea. It's clear from any number of real-world examples that whatever the interest is, it's possible to turn it into a successful business with hard work and determination. After reading Chapter 6, you might already have a solid idea of something you're passionate or very knowledgeable about. You might even have a business plan. But what do you do next?

Making your business plan
Building something from scratch can be super exciting and it's easy to get carried away in all the fun elements of creating something new,

but working on a business plan is the first step and will help you think realistically, objectively and unemotionally about your business.

A business plan is crucial because it will highlight how much money you need to design, plan and market your business. You don't need anything fancy – a good spreadsheet outlining all your plans and research is a really great start.

Your plan should answer the following questions:

- Who is your target market – that is, who will actually buy your product or service?
- Where will you run the business from?
- What are your branding, logos, website and social media handles?
- How much will it cost to start? (See section 7.2 for more)
- Where will you source the products or equipment you need to offer your service?
- How many products or service packages will you launch? At what point will you expand this?
- How will you market your business?
- What will postage and packaging entail if delivery is required, or how much will you need to set aside for travel if you are leaving home to help others?

It is always a good idea to talk to a consultant or seek advice from people you know in the industry or field you're moving into. Gather all the information you need at this stage to decide whether or not a business is what you want, and if you really believe you can commit to the hard work and financial investment required to make it successful.

Supply and demand

One of the first principles of any business is to offer something that people want or need. Thinking about whether people need or want the product or service you are passionate about is vital. Who else is offering the same service? Are they always doing a roaring trade and making a ton of sales? Do they have waiting lists of customers or clients? Are products on back order because they've sold out?

If you've answered yes to any of those questions, there is definitely room for another player (you!) to step in for a slice of the pie.

If what you have to offer is new and no one else is doing it, making it or selling it, you will be the groundbreaker who gets to test and measure demand. Before you launch into full-blown production, however, test the waters with people you know and trust. It's really as simple as asking the question, 'What do you think of this?' If their feedback isn't all rainbows and unicorns, take their comments on board (to an extent) and see if there are small changes that will make it even better – and increase demand for your offering.

Consider the following questions:
- Who will buy your product or service?
- Why would they buy it?
- Why would customers/clients choose you, specifically?
- Who is your ideal customer?
- Is it a 'minimum viable product'? By this, I mean does your product or service have enough features to satisfy early customers and provide feedback for future product development?

Remember not to be put off if there are a number of people offering the same or similar product or service – that means there is demand for it, after all. Take mobile hairdressers for example – there are often multiple mobile hair services in every suburb, and while they may allow some healthy competition for clients, they often co-exist quite happily because there is enough demand that they can share the load and still make great money. That said, the best way to stand out from the crowd is to find your niche and focus most of your marketing on what only you can offer. Read on for more.

Finding a niche product or service

What is a niche? It's a point of difference that sets you apart from everyone else. It is finding a gap in the market that you can take advantage of. To use the mobile hairdresser example again, while every hairdresser might offer cuts and colours, one might use certified organic products, which sets them apart. This niche would attract people with allergies or sensitivities, or people who keen to live an organic lifestyle.

To use a product example, if you were to import toys wholesale to sell online, you would be one of thousands doing the same thing. But what if you began grouping collections of toys together and selling them as themed showbags or activity packs? That way you would become a niche offering that might appeal to young fans of those themes (for example, based on TV shows, movies or book characters), and attracting parents who are on the hunt for the perfect birthday or Christmas gift for their mini fanatic.

Finding a niche can be a fun exercise because you can think outside the box. You'd be surprised how one small point of difference can morph into extra cashola.

How to discover your core demographic

You might think that your product or service is useful for everyone, and that may be the case. But it's a logistical nightmare trying to market your business to 'everyone'. Instead, think about who your ideal customer is. This doesn't mean that you *only* sell to this ideal customer, but you will find that by talking directly to your core demographic, you will attract people from other demographics by default. This will save you wasting your time and marketing budget trying to lure in people who have no interest in what you have to offer. Instead, every second and every cent spent on your marketing counts because you're speaking the language of the people who will actually connect with your offering.

To narrow down your ideal customer, consider the following questions as they relate to your product or service. Some of them may seem irrelevant, but give your best guess if you are unsure. It will all go towards building your ideal customer profile:

- Do they identify as male, female or non-binary?
- How old are they?
- What is their relationship status?
- Do they have children?

- Do they work in a particular industry?
- Do they have particular interests?
- Are they high earners or on a low income?
- What are their key values?
- What features will be important to them?
- What have they been struggling with that you can fix?

Keep all of this in mind when developing your business and, most importantly, when you venture into the marketing space. This will ensure you are reaching the right people with the message they want to hear, making it more likely your products or services will be in demand.

7.2 Think hard about start-up costs

There was a time when starting your own business required a whole lot of capital and probably a loan. Now, many businesses get by with what they have on hand, saving money by sourcing things they need in a clever way. Debt is a difficult beast, so I would advise you to think long and hard before you take out a loan for your business.

Your business plan will show you precisely how much money is needed to start your business but remember, you can start small. Try not to feel the pressure to launch with your grand plan at the start – you can build up to it once you've made some initial sales and got the ball rolling.

If you're fortunate enough to have capital available to you, all you need to do is figure out what you can achieve with your budget and get started. If the projected cost is much higher than the money you have available, then you need to revise your plan and take on a new perspective. Can you do most of it yourself? Can you procure the materials or products more cheaply? Are there different ways you can offer your service without the need for expensive equipment? These and many more questions will help you cut down costs and may change your business scope.

If there's no other way around it, and you're highly confident about your idea and your business plan, you can try getting investors, getting a loan or crowdfunding your start-up. Raising the money you need to launch a start-up business label can be tricky. Financial institutions regard fledgling businesses as high-risk ventures and will only lend money if you have collateral such as real estate, so this is not the path I recommend for most small business start-ups.

7.3 Determine the legal structure of your business

Before registering the business, you need to choose the most fitting business structure. For example, if you plan to be accountable for all legal obligations and debts personally, you can go ahead as a sole trader. If you have a business partner, a partnership would have you and your partner jointly responsible for the liabilities of your business. There are other corporate structures where the company becomes a separate legal entity from the owners, which means the company can assume liability, own property, enter into contracts or pay taxes.

It can get quite complex, so I recommend researching the Australian Taxation Office (ATO) website to help figure out which type of business is best for your future objectives as well as current needs. You could also make an appointment with an accountant, who will be able to tell you the best way to set up your business, and will assist in setting it up for you. Depending on your specific circumstances, you may also wish to seek legal advice.

7.4 Register for an ABN

An Australian Business Number (ABN) is a unique 11-digit identification number for your business. This is used when dealing with other businesses and to identify yourself to the tax department. With an ABN you can:
- Purchase an Australian domain name (.com.au).
- Confirm your business identity to others when ordering and invoicing.

- Easily identify your company to government agencies.
- Claim GST and energy grant credits.

Not all businesses need an ABN, but it really is advisable. Without an ABN, other businesses need to withhold up to 47% of any money they pay you for taxation purposes – ouch! You also cannot claim business expenses at tax time without an ABN, such as car expenses including fuel, internet, phone, electricity and gas, whereas you can often claim a portion of those if they are a part of operating your business.

Not everyone is entitled to an ABN. When you apply via the Australian Business Register you will be asked a series of questions to determine if you are eligible. One common distinction that makes or breaks an ABN application is determining whether you are an employee or a contractor. An employee is not entitled to an ABN, but a contractor (or freelancer) is. More information on eligibility can be found on the Australian Taxation Office and Australian Business Register sites.

Before you get started with your application, read the next section about choosing your business name, as you might want to use it immediately for your ABN.

If you qualify for an ABN, the next step is to apply for the number. Stay on the Australian Business Register site and fill in your details. Completing the form can take about 20 minutes.

The online form will require you to provide:
- Your details
- Business information
- Associate details
- Activities of the business
- Reasons for the application

Once you've submitted your application, you will be notified of whether you have been successful, or need to provide more information, or if your application has been refused. If your application has been successful, you then have the opportunity to continue on and apply for other business registrations depending on the status of your ABN application and the type of entity your business is.

All of this can be confusing for beginners, so talk to your accountant, who can help you set it up correctly and legally.

7.5 Choose and register your business name

Choosing a business name – the name under which the business will run – can be harder than it sounds because you need to have something individual and different to everyone else's; you also want something catchy, appealing and that relates to your product or service. Sure, you can use your own name if you want to – and this can be really appropriate for some types of businesses – but chances are you'll want a specific business name.

When choosing your name, you need to consider things like domain names, email addresses, trademarks . . . the list goes on! The best thing to do before worrying about any of these is to make a list of a few names that you like and that relate to what your business is all about. The more you can come up with, the better, as you may find several of them are already taken or too similar to what someone else has to distinguish yourself as a separate entity. Compromise and creativity may be necessary. I talk about choosing a domain name later in this chapter (see section 7.7), so you might like to skip ahead to check that out – some of those considerations may factor in here.

Once you have your list, it's time to start researching. Here are several searches that are worth doing:

- Google all the names you're thinking of. See if anyone similar pops up, even in other countries, as this may affect things like copyright, trademarks and domain names, just to name a few. Even if these issues seem a long way off, don't limit yourself – you never know how big your business could grow!
- Check out the ASIC (Australian Securities & Investments Commission) website at www.asic.gov.au. Search the database of business names in Australia and find out if your favourites are available.
- Jump on one of the many website domain name registry services. Search for domains that will match your business name. It's best to

check that both .com and .com.au options are available as buying both will ensure you get the majority of your potential website traffic. Think how many times you've forgotten the .au on a website – if forgetting this sends your potential customers to another website, you could be losing out. Depending on what kind of business you're running, you can also get .net, .net.au, .org and more. Common domain name businesses include Crazy Domains, GoDaddy, Hover and Name.com.

- If you're going to use a provider like Gmail for email, check that out too. Make sure you can get addresses you're happy with that match up with your business. Otherwise, you can always get email through the provider that hosts your website, but this is likely to cost more.
- Search for the name you plan to use on Facebook too, to make sure it's not already being used by someone, as well as Instagram, Twitter, TikTok and any other social media platform you plan on using for advertising and exposure. In huge networks such as these, it is important to be as unique as possible so you're easy to find and interact with.

Once you've taken all these steps and have figured out which names from your list are unique and appropriate, it's time to jump in with both feet and fill out your registration form to get your very own business name. First, you need to sign up for an ASIC account, then proceed to register your chosen business name. This should take about 20 minutes. When you pay to register your business name, you have a choice of paying for one year or three years. One year will set you back $37 and three years $87 at the time of writing. It's worth noting that if your registration application is unsuccessful, you don't get your money back.

7.6 Set up a business bank account

It's a good idea to have a separate account for business finances to keep things simple. This is not mandatory if you're in a partnership or sole proprietorship, but it's strongly recommended, because you have to keep clear and verifiable accounts for taxation and auditing purposes. A very basic business bank account is pretty straightforward to set up with your local bank. You will just need all the details from your accountant. Don't be scared to call your bank or accountant and ask for direction or help with choosing banking products that are right for your situation – they do this all day every day, and are there to help.

Money management should be one of your key skills as a business owner. When your business starts to grow, it can be difficult to keep track of your orders, stock levels, delivery and everything else. A spreadsheet won't cut it, and you'll need to find an accounting and stock tracking system to manage production, inventory, costing, orders and more. Once you build up cashflow in your business, you can outsource the managing of these components to others if you are not a numbers person. Until then, it's important not to neglect this vital component, or you could find yourself in hot water.

7.7 Buy your domain name

It doesn't matter whether the business will be online or a bricks-and-mortar store – in this day and age, you will need a website, which means securing a domain name. This is the unique online address where people can find you. For example, the name of my blog is Stay at Home Mum and my domain name is www.stayathomemum.com.au. I also own www.stayathomemum.com, which I redirect to my .com.au site because people can look for both.

You should have already done some research in this department when you were choosing your business name, so now you can proceed with the option you chose. To register the domain name, head to the Domain Administration site (www.auda.org.au) for links to resellers and registers, and to confirm current options and fees. This is where you can also use the domain name to create email and social media accounts for the business.

Buying a domain name is pretty cheap to do. Here in Australia if you buy a .com.au domain name, you need to register it for at least one year, sometimes two. After this period of time, your domain name will expire, and you'll need to pay additional fees to continue ownership. It's always best to purchase a domain name in the country where you live. If your mind is set on a particular website name and you notice that the domain name isn't available but isn't being used by whoever owns it, you can always ask the person who owns it if they wish to sell it to you. Sometimes they will demand a ridiculous amount, but it's certainly worth trying if you have your heart set on that name. Remember, the worst thing they can say is no.

7.8 Branding

Now is one of my favourite parts: figuring out your branding! Every business needs a logo, and while you might update it in a few years, you want to choose something that's going to last. This is the image that your customers will associate with your brand, so don't rush it.

If you aren't artistically minded, make some notes about what you want and head to places like Fiverr.com or 99designs.com.au to find someone you can pay to create a logo for you. You can also design a simple logo on programs like Canva; however, be aware that everyone else can do this too, so your end product may not look completely original.

Business cards

Once you have a logo, you can start using it. The first thing I recommend is to order a run of business cards. These might seem so 1990s, but they're still a very important tool for a lot of businesses, no matter the size. Even though online advertising is important, many businesses still do a lot of their customer networking through word of mouth. For this kind of networking, having business cards is really essential as it allows you to market yourself and your business wherever you go. For example, if you're starting out with a market stall, many people will grab a card if they like your work but aren't ready to commit on the spot. Being able to hand a new contact all your details in one simple transaction makes the relatively inexpensive outlay worth it.

There are numerous online companies that offer simple business card templates that you can use, including Canva, which I've already mentioned a few times, and getting them printed is relatively affordable. Every card should have the following:

- Your name
- The position you hold in the business
- Your business name
- Your mobile phone number
- Your email address
- Your website

Other items you can include if they are important to your business:

- Your postal or business address
- Award wins

Although the primary purpose of your business card is to clearly and simply provide your contact information, there's nothing wrong with making it cute or clever as well – after all, business cards are a reflection of both you and your brand. If you want something a bit left-of-centre, here are some ideas:

- Include a QR code on the back that people can scan to go straight to a landing page on your website with all your information.
- Instead of printing your information landscape like most traditional business cards, consider printing them portrait. This stands out from the crowd, but still looks classy.
- Print on both sides of the card. If people already have your card, you may as well put all the space to good use, so fill the back with something about your website or brand.

Quality and price

Some business cards out there *feel* cheap, which you want to avoid, but then at the other end of the spectrum are the expensive, thick, beautiful business cards that just seem like a waste of money. If you can, go for something in between – choose a good-quality card stock, and perhaps some nice embossing. These days, business cards are pretty inexpensive – you can easily get 250 business cards for under $10. But for just a few dollars extra, you can upgrade your business card to feel a whole lot nicer.

Here are some options for affordable design and printing:

- Vistaprint – a fast, low-cost provider of not just business cards but any initial printing work that a new small business might need. They have a massive selection of marketing materials to choose from. When it comes to business cards, they even have templates to use if you don't yet have a logo or look for your small business.
- Udesignit offers 100 very basic business cards for only $10. Perfect for business start-ups or low budgets.
- MOO.com has lots of quirky options for business cards. Want a square business card? Maybe mini business cards, or even cotton business cards made from recycled T-shirts? I really love their range as it's just so different and gorgeous.
- Jukebox Print has a vast range of business card options, including bamboo, eco-friendly, cannabis, wooden, sparkle, cotton, cork and gold-foiled.

Quantity

If these are your very first business cards, order the smallest amount you can. After all, you may change your mind about your logo or styling once you're established in business, or realise you've forgotten something your customers really want to know. Once you know you'll stick with your branding for the long haul, then you can look at getting larger quantities.

7.9 Look at insurance

Purchasing insurance for your business is crucial. Dealing with unforeseen incidents like customer lawsuits, theft or property damage can be very expensive, and you need to be assured that your business is protected. If you employ workers, workers compensation insurance is a mandatory requirement for employers in Australia; the premium rate will depend on the nature of the company's main business.

If you aren't too sure about what insurances you need, talk to a few insurance agencies and then compare notes. You don't want to spend too much on insurance that you can't afford – just the right insurance to cover your arse in case something goes wrong! There are also business insurance brokers out there who can do all of the legwork for you.

Hot tip: If you use a business insurance brokers, be sure that you vet them first to be confident that they have access to a wide range of insurance providers and aren't loyal to just one or two companies.

7.10 Register for GST

Goods and services tax, or GST, is a tax of 10% on most goods, services and other items sold or consumed in Australia. Business.gov.au states that 'As a business owner, it's your responsibility to register for GST if your turnover exceeds the $75,000 threshold or is likely to exceed it. The ATO advises that if you've just started a new business and expect it to earn $75,000 or more in its first year of operation, you should register for GST.' Most new small businesses are unlikely to earn that much in their first year, so you may well be able to skip this for the time being.

I'm not going to go into too much detail here because a) it's boring and b) this is where you get your accountant to give you a hand – that's what they are there for.

7.11 Project management and planning your time

So that's it – you've set up your brand-new business! But there's a couple more steps I recommend to make your life easier and to help look after yourself in your new business life.

Now that you're moving towards beginning an exciting new life in your fledgling business, it's important to take some time to think about the practical realities of project management before you start. There are so many project management and time-planning apps available online now: I highly recommend you consider them. Some have a membership or sign-up fee, but they may well be worth the investment. If you ensure that every job that needs to be done is entered into the program, this in turn ensures that the job gets done – and on time. It's also great to have a tool like this if you're working with another person, as you can delegate jobs to them and vice versa.

Some project management tools include:

- Basecamp
- Asana
- Podio
- Workzone
- Scoro
- Workbook

There are literally thousands of them – and many can be downloaded as an app for your phone. Have a look at the pros and cons of each to find the one that will suit you best. Also see Chapter 13 for more apps that can help your business.

Find yourself some company

Working from home can sometimes be lonely, even if the kids are underfoot. I highly recommend you join a few online business groups so you can talk to others who are on the same journey as you, and to ask for help or guidance where and when you need it.

Some Facebook groups for small businesses include:

- Like Minded Bitches Drinking Wine

- Women in Australian Small Business
- The Lady Startup Lounge
- Girls in Business

Also consider reaching out to someone you admire and see if they'll offer you any advice, or even ask if they are keen to mentor you. Remember, if you don't ask, you don't get!

Make time for yourself too

Gah – all that work on your business, and now you need to work on yourself? Well, yes! Nothing should ever make you take yourself for granted. Even with all the hustle and bustle of life and business, at the end of the day you have to take care of yourself so you don't eventually burn out. Your body is your own investment. Working at night may be necessary sometimes for your business, but try not to make a habit of it – it will rob you of energy and wellbeing, and this won't do you *or* your business any favours in the long run.

Be mindful of your health. Eat regularly. Drink water. Do some exercise when you can. Just do everything that will keep you sane. You can also treat yourself once in a while. The bottom line is, you need to value and love yourself if your business is to succeed.

Conclusion

As you can see, before you jump into any business endeavour, it's essential to do your research and homework. There's a lot that goes into launching a business, and considering its structure and tax ramifications is just the first of many steps you need to take. But they are just that – steps you can take one at a time, following the guide I've laid out in this chapter – and with the assistance of experts such as accountants, I know you can do it!

Chapter 8

Selling stuff online

Since selling physical products online is a huge part of most businesses these days, I want to focus on this in this chapter. If your business is only operating in an online space, you are still bound by the same legal requirements and basic principles of setting up a business of any kind.

If you want to create a new product or something unique that isn't already readily available, you can pour your time and creativity into making it yourself, or you can seek out companies that have white labelling options where they manufacture the product for you ready to rebrand as your own. This chapter covers all of your options so you can see what would work best for your business model.

8.1 What are the best products to sell online?

It's all well and good to have a product that you love and want to sell online – in fact, finding a great product to sell is how most people get into small business in the first place – but have you considered the logistics of your choice? And could you choose something along the same lines that will be easier to manage? Finding a single product that ticks all the 'perfect product' boxes is near impossible. However, there are certainly important issues to consider when choosing a product.

Shipping and handling

Selling your own product or even other people's products can be very lucrative, but take the time to answer the following questions before you start, or you might find you've got a product to ship and handle that's more trouble than it's worth:

- Is the product lightweight, heavy or fragile? This will affect how easy and cheap it is to post. Will the cost of postage cut into your profits?
- How many product lines will you have?
- Will your product require specialised packaging?
- Will you ship internationally? Are there special rules about mailing your item?
- Is there an additional cost to send your product through customs?
- Is your product relatively cheap to make or buy, but expensive to ship? This can put off many buyers who would prefer to find an alternative closer to where they live.
- Are there ways to make your product lighter, or can you reconfigure the packaging so it can be sent more cheaply?
- Can you negotiate delivery with a local courier?

Competition

Is the product unique to you and your online store or are there thousands of sellers selling the exact same product? If you need to compete with all those other sellers, is there a way to make your product different or stand out from the crowd? Can you adapt the product to make it unique?

What is your price point?

Are you selling your item for between $10 and $200? Apparently (this is according to the internet, so it must be true!), people are more likely to buy a product if it is priced between $10 and $200. It has become the 'proven' sweet spot. Luckily, the majority of products sold online typically fall into this price range.

Is it a seasonal product?

Beach towels are gorgeous and make a fantastic online product, but they are only likely to sell in summer. Think carefully about your product and whether it will be have seasonal ups and downs, because that will mean you have few or no customers for six months of the year.

Is the product consumable?

Will the customer use the product up, so they have to return to your online store for more of it? Consumable products are a great way to get repeat business. Examples of consumable products include:

- Make-up and skincare
- Gourmet food
- Cleaning products
- Paint and craft supplies
- Printer ink

8.2 Packaging and delivery

Once you have a great idea for a product, the next step is to work out how best to package and ship that product.

Packaging

Packaging is not only about getting your product to the customer safely (important though that is!), but is also a way to show off your brand. This is your customer's first impression of the product they've bought from you, so you want to aim for beautiful but cost-effective packaging that reflects your brand, whether that be via colours, style or eco-friendliness.

Keep in mind that packaging does generally end up in the bin, so try to keep the cost down where possible while making it a fun and exciting experience to receive and open packages from you. And of course the packaging should reflect the product – do you need bubblewrap to keep it safe, or perhaps you want it to feel a little bit luxurious with tissue paper and ribbon. High-end products will require packaging that reflects their luxury status, while more utilitarian products will be best served by practical, no-fuss packaging.

Types of packaging include (but aren't limited to):

- Cardboard boxes
- Gift boxes
- Poly bags
- Foil bags
- Plastic boxes

Hot tip: You can pick up beautiful boxes at discount stores such as The Reject Shop!

Other ideas for making your parcels special could be to include a handwritten note thanking the recipient for their purchase or to use a stamp with your logo for a handmade feel.

Delivery

Nowadays we aren't just limited to Australia Post when it comes to sending our items around Australia and the world – we have multiple options. Not all of the following are available in all areas, but do some research to see if they're competitively priced for your needs:

- Australia Post
- Sendle
- WizMe
- Pack & Send
- Smart Send
- E-Go
- Parcel Connect

8.3 Your online store

Using all the available tools to sell your product online might mean going beyond your free social media accounts into a dedicated online space – by this, I mean setting up your own website to sell your product. Sure, you can sell your products or services from your Facebook page or Instagram account, but remember that no social media channel really belongs to you, so your business will be affected by any changes to those social media platforms. This is also true of third-party sites you might choose to sell through, which we'll look at on page 151.

By creating your own website, you have a real, saleable asset and you have almost full control over it. If you decide you no longer want to run your business, you can sell your store, ideally for a profit, ensuring all that work you've put into your shop gives you a good return. Legally, you cannot 'sell' a Facebook page, so that's another advantage to having your own website. You don't need to spend a lot of money to get something up and running, and it's not as hard as you might think. Let me show you how to get started.

Choosing a website platform

When considering where to base your website, you need to think about what you actually want that website to do. Given that this chapter is about selling online, you probably need it to have a shop – known as an e-commerce function. Do you also want to blog, and ideally monetise your site? Otherwise, you might just need an online presence to have a good overview of your business and what you offer for customers. Asking yourself these questions will help you choose the right website on the right platform – a bit of planning now will go a long way in saving you time and money down the track. I discuss blogging in more detail in Chapter 10 with information about choosing a host and platform for your website but here I'll focus on building an online store.

Choosing an e-commerce platform

If you're searching for a good shopping e-commerce platform to run your new online store, you have no doubt heard about at least a few of the big names you'll see below.

Choosing something popular is usually the way people go when choosing a platform for their online store, but it isn't necessarily the best option. There are many factors to consider when choosing a platform that best suits your product, your budget and – most importantly – your audience. Make sure you evaluate the features of each platform carefully so your needs are met.

I'll outline some e-commerce platforms available at the time of writing, including the pros and cons of each, and list their pricing (because let's face it, cost is important).

Shopify

There's a good reason why Shopify is one of the most recommended platforms for anyone who wants to get started in the e-commerce sector. It's popular with small shop owners because it's specifically designed for this niche market.

The Basic plan for Shopify starts from US$29 per month, while the advanced package will set you back US$299 per month. There is also a Shopify Lite version that allows you to sell on Facebook and add any products to a website or blog. Shopify Lite starts at US$9 per month, which is much more affordable for small businesses starting out.

Shopify has the most features of all the e-commerce sites we'll be discussing, but it can take a while to learn the ropes. If you're busy and time-poor, this can be frustrating. However, if you are serious about your small business and willing to take your time to learn how to use it properly, it is certainly worth the investment!

Pros:

• Shopify makes it easy and simple to expand the abilities of any default web store.

- It provides a good selection of apps and professional themes (important parts of your website), which is more than any of its competitors.
- Shopify sends a reminder to customers who didn't check out and allows the recovery of an abandoned cart.
- You can upload an almost unlimited number of products.
- Shopify can be easily integrated with the systems of fulfilment centres, shipping carriers and dropshipping companies, although this is currently more popular in the United States than Australia.
- It also provides a mobile app for both managing your store and accepting payments.
- It offers a point-of-sale system for handling transactions in a physical shop or market stall.
- The Shopify Experts tool can help you set up your store.
  Cons:
- Shopify costs money, both in individual transaction processing fees and a monthly subscription fee.
- Shopify is uniquely and proprietarily coded, which can delay managing your store and increase maintenance costs.

Volusion

Volusion is a fully cloud-based e-commerce store that offers all the basic functions of running an online store. Deciding whether to use Volusion comes down to whether or not you feel comfortable editing the CSS and HTML code (and if you don't know what that means, this isn't the platform for you!). With Volusion, some coding is necessary if you want to optimise your template.

Volusion (like Shopify) comes with both an iOS and Android app so you can check your online store when you're on the go. You can also connect it to social media.

Having owned both a Shopify store and a Volusion-based store, I found Volusion easier to use. But unless you have tech knowledge, you will need to work with a good developer to set everything up, which can get expensive.

Pros:

- Volusion's interface is intuitive to use.
- It provides many useful features such as an in-built rewards program, coupon capability, affiliate set-up, gift certificates and advanced shipping.
- The shopping platform comes with integrating inventory.
- The customer support for this program is second to none.

Cons:

- The program has a complicated fee structure that includes many secondary costs, which can make it an expensive choice.
- Users are forced to pay for SSL (encryption of data, non-negotiable for an e-commerce site).
- For those who would need a premium template, the price tag is very high!

WooCommerce

This site goes hand in hand with WordPress websites. In fact, 28% of all e-commerce websites are a WooCommerce shop – not too shabby. One advantage is that it's built for both real products and digital downloads (for example, ebooks). It is supported by an app and doesn't require any custom coding.

If you're just dipping your toes into the e-commerce world and have no funds to invest, then this could be a great platform for you. However, it may not do everything you want it to, and if your business is here to stay, changing over to a more scalable platform might be difficult.

Pros:

- WooCommerce is a free plug-in that is available alongside WordPress.
- Out of the box, this online shopping platform comes with a number of ready-to-go features, including coupon codes and email marketing.

Cons:

- The software is not as comprehensive and feature-rich as other platforms.

- In order to work, it requires you to have a functioning WordPress website.
- WooCommerce may require some premium upgrades if you want additional functions.

BigCommerce

This is a fully integrated e-commerce website. You don't need Word-Press to plug in – it's a stand-alone platform. There are loads of beautiful templates to choose from, the platform is fully customisable (and code-free, which is good for the likes of us who have no tech knowledge). If you're unhappy with your current e-commerce platform, BigCommerce makes it easy to import all the information over.

BigCommerce allows you to sell on eBay and Facebook as well as implement a 'buy' button on images. It is also very Google friendly, with all images uploaded into your BigCommerce store featuring in the Google search.

Basically, BigCommerce is a good, easy-to-use platform that's affordable and scalable. It doesn't have everything, but has most of what e-commerce stores require. That's a thumbs up from me!

Pros:
- BigCommerce comes with great management tools, including order management, product management, reports, analytics and more.
- It provides a marketing module with coupons, AdWords integration and more.
- For the number of features provided, BigCommerce is relatively inexpensive.
- The online shopping platform provides 24/7 customer support.
- Your store can be integrated with various apps and platforms such as QuickBooks, Facebook, eBay, MailChimp, and a lot more.
- Its shopping cart can handle multiple currencies.

Cons:
- The premium themes are expensive.
- You cannot easily adjust the homepage.

- The homepage carousel is a bit hard to use.
- The design adjustment doesn't always work as predicted.

8.4 Sell through third-party sites

No matter what sort of product or service you have, you need a platform of some kind to sell your stuff. If you don't want to have your own website, you can look at selling via a third-party site. There are quite a few different selling platforms available. Sure, most of them charge you a fee to list your product and many take a percentage of your sales as commission, but they also get eyeballs on your product because they're established sites with regular traffic – and the more eyeballs on your product, the more you will sell. Even if you have your own website, you might still consider using a third-party site while you're broadening your reach.

Some of the most popular general selling platforms are:

- eBay
- Gumtree
- Facebook Marketplace
- Amazon
- Etsy
- Madeit

Hot tips for using third-party platforms

When selling through these platforms, you'll need to upload each product individually. So step one is to ensure you have a fantastic main image of your product, and take at least four more clear photographs from different angles.

Ensure that the write-up about the product is clear, descriptive and thorough. If you aren't sure about your sales copy, look at other listings of similar items to get a feel for the information you need to provide. If you have honest friends and family members, have them look over your sales copy to see if they have any questions about the product so you can include information you may have inadvertently missed.

Each platform has different fee structures, so make sure you read all the terms and conditions before setting your prices so you can build in the fees.

> **Tip:** Offering free postage and building this cost into the price will ensure more sales than adding postage on top.

8.5 Email lists

Now, let's turn to the controversial matter of email lists and whether or not this is a good option for your business. An email list is all the people who you sent emails to advertising your product or service. People need to sign up to your email list – you can't just spam anyone you like.

Most online 'experts' say that email is the best place to get customers interested in your products. Personally, I think email lists are so ten years ago, and apart from letting your customers know about special deals, or unless your brand has a cult following, they're a waste of time for most small business start-ups. Think about it – when was the last time you actually took the time to open and read an email that didn't have '50% off sale!' in the subject line?

Most people are too busy to actually read the many emails they receive and just skim their inbox to see what to delete. The open rate across all industries is just 21.33% (per Mailchimp). So if you have 100 email subscribers, only 21 people will open the email. Of those 21 people, only 3% will click on an item – and an even smaller percentage actually buy something. That is a whole lot of work for nearly nothing in return.

If you want to set up an email list, by all means do so. But don't put excessive time or energy into the process when you could be creating awesome content for your website or social media presence, which will get eyeballs on your product or service, and be more likely to result in sales. Just remember that customers need to opt in to your mailing list but also have the option to unsubscribe if they no longer want to receive mail from you, as per Australian spam laws.

8.6 Import products from overseas

Let's turn now to the all-important area of sourcing products for your online store if you're not producing your own. Whatever the item is that you want to sell, you need to find a reputable supplier, so you'll need to do some research, looking into any importing laws, quarantine and customs requirements and government regulations.

Many websites can assist you with finding a supplier, or you can use some of the major overseas shopping sites such as SaleHoo or AliExpress that will help you import from China.

Before you spend a huge amount of money on importing goods, always dip your toe in the pond by getting a sample of the product you want to sell first so you can make sure the quality of the product is what you expect. Consider the shipping time, ease of communication and the packaging it arrives in as well. If you can wait for products to be delivered, importing products from overseas can be a huge cost-saving opportunity, though you need to factor in any additional costs such as import duty taxes and GST.

Check that you are allowed to import the particular product you're looking at, as there is a long list of prohibited goods. They include:
- Drugs, medicines and therapeutic substances
- Animals and plants
- Weapons
- Any fur products
- Cosmetics that contain toxic materials
- Items of cultural heritage

A customs broker can advise you of any additional costs or charges that may be incurred with importing goods.

8.7 Dropshipping

Dropshipping is where you advertise a product, sell the product to the consumer, then the *supplier* delivers the goods directly to the consumer rather than *you* needing to physically handle the product and post it out. This is the perfect business model, don't you think? No need to do anything other than build a website, pick the products and their supplier, and finally advertise your products. However, you will still need to focus on customer service and dealing with any queries or problems that potential and current customers might have.

Make sure you choose companies with a good reputation and previous experience in dropshipping, because some dropshippers might not deliver the product they promised to supply. It's easy to take advantage of you if you've never seen the product in person, so always get a sample and follow up to ensure that's what your customers are getting too. Some dropshippers show you a picture of the product you think you're selling, but send the customer something completely different.

Make sure that you can easily communicate with them via phone or email. One way to confirm how good a potential dropshipper is to go undercover. Order a few test products to be sent to your house. This way you can evaluate both the quality of the products and how well the business communicates with the customer. If you're happy with the test products, then you can negotiate a quote for the number of products you need. I've used dropshipping companies to sell T-shirts, garden supplies and clothing, and it's been a great experience. I'll share with you some pros and cons I've found along the way.

Advantages of dropshipping:

- Allows you to offer good-quality, popular products so you don't need to produce them yourself.
- You can quickly change the type or style of products that you're selling.
- Profits on products are usually around 15–20%, or more.
- There is no financial outlay for stock – you only pay the supplier when your customer pays.

- There is no need to store stock – the supplier keeps all stock at their warehouse.
- There is no handling or postage – the dropshipper is responsible for all postage.
- For an extra cost you can send the dropshipper stickers and other packaging items printed with your logo so that the products look like they come from you. When doing your research, enquire what the extra costs would be to have your own packaging.
Negatives of dropshipping:
- One thing you really must consider with dropshipping is that your postage time will be significantly longer if your supplier is not local. You can either disclose to the customer how long their item will take to deliver, or find a local dropshipper to make postage faster.
- If suppliers are not local, it might be harder to communicate with them. It's wise to do a few tests to see which dropshipper can offer the best communication. You as the business owner, and your customers, will need information about products as well as how the supplier handles returns. You need to ensure that phone and email communication is accessible and handled within a reasonable timeframe.
- Dropshipping is not a business where you just list products on a website and then they sell themselves. You need to put in a lot of time to market and advertise your goods and to be available for your customers. Good customer service can make the difference between a business that is successful and one that isn't.
- You might feel that you need to earn more profit for all your hard work. To help boost your profits, you can try to negotiate a cheaper price per unit with your supplier, and increase the cost per product to your customer, but this is always a balancing act.

How to set up a dropshipping store

Setting up a dropshipping store is super easy – I think you'll be pleasantly surprised at how simple it is! Here's how:

1. Set up an e-commerce platform that allows for dropshipping (see earlier in this chapter). For the purposes of this walk-through, let's say you sign up for Shopify, perhaps with the free trial on offer.
2. Now you have your Shopify store, activate the Oberlo and Modalyst apps. Note that there is a fee to use these apps.
3. Select your dropshipper or shippers of choice, and add the products to your Shopify store.
4. Next, promote your shop and sell your products. As simple as that!

The Oberlo and Modalyst apps are a must for me even though there is a fee involved, because they plug in seamlessly with Shopify stores to help you find products. Oberlo also allows you to search various dropshippers or via a certain product; you can even narrow the search to a certain country. I've used Oberlo and love how it helps curate and promote my products.

Another thing I love is the AliExpress Google Chrome Extension (AliDropship). From the AliExpress website, click the little blue paperclip icon on the product, and if you have Oberlo open at the same time this automatically adds the product to Oberlo, where you can edit it, adding images, text, shipping and prices. Once happy you can push it live to your Shopify store. Believe me, it's easy!

Pre-made dropshipping websites

If you want to start testing the dropshipping waters, an inexpensive option is to use a pre-made dropshipping website. These templates look very professional and as you know by now, stunning sites help to win over customers. There are a few places that make inexpensive readymade dropshipping websites which are definitely worth a look. Here are some of my faves.

DropshipForSale

This has affordable and stylish templates for your new dropshipping business. You can pick from a starter site, a premium site or a custom site. Have a look at its ready-made websites to see all the niche topics out there; for example, Electronics & Gadgets, Hair & Wig, Fresh Coffee, Pet, Make-up & Teeth Whitening, Baby Store.

DropshipMe

This platform provides ready-built dropshipping stores and also does all the research to ensure the products you choose will sell well. Picking your products is the hardest thing, so if you can get some extra help, why not? Once you've picked your winning products, all you need to do is market them. DropshipMe has beautiful photography to help sell your products, so this is a must-have! There is a free version, which lets you add 50 products. If you need more, you can move to a paid plan.

Major dropshipping companies

Let's look at the major dropshipping companies available to Australia. They offer a multitude of products but you generally need to become a member to see all their products. While I've done my best to recommend legitimate companies (with prices correct at the time of writing), always do your homework before parting with any cash!

Professional dropshipping companies take a small percentage of every sale for their services, but you have access to literally millions of products, which gives you so many options about what you choose to sell. Here are some companies to look at.

Worldwide Brands

Worldwide Brands doesn't actually offer dropshipping products, but it provides a list of suppliers for a fee. It's a who's who of dropshipping – having a list of who to contact is sometimes half the battle.

SaleHoo

This has an amazing selection of products for dropshippers – their list is *huge*. You can choose between a yearly US$67 membership or US$127 lifetime access. SaleHoo has a 60-day guarantee in case you're not completely satisfied. The membership gets you access to their drop-shipping supplier directory, members forum and all the research that will help you become a successful dropshipper.

SaleHoo has more quality products for dropshipping than most, with over two million products and brands. It has been around since 2005, so it's one of the longest running dropshipping companies. All the SaleHoo sellers are real and authorised distributors of the products you are buying.

Factory Fast

Factory Fast is Australian owned and operated, so getting products to your customers will be quicker than coming from overseas. Not only does it dropship, you can also become a reseller of its products. There's no membership fee, and it stocks so many amazing products that you might not have thought of selling, including products for DIY and renovation, furniture, games, outdoor furniture, toys, sports and fitness, pet supplies, home entertainment, travel goods, baby products and so forth.

Simply Wholesale

Simply Wholesale dropships electronics, home and garden, health, homewares, beauty products, tools and equipment. It offers over 100,000 products and free shipping Australia-wide, and has an easy 14-day returns policy.

Wholesale2b

Wholesale2b is not based in Australia, but does offer dropshipping here and has warehouses all over the world. There are over one million dropshipping products to choose from (one of the world's largest drop-shipping companies). If you are really serious about starting a small business doing dropshipping, sign up for one of their plans that inte-grates with Shopify and WooCommerce – or they can even help you assemble your very own dropshipping website.

You can sign up for a free seven-day trial, after which you're charged US$29.99 if connecting to a Shopify website. For the trial plan and the monthly plan, you can import 10,000 products. That's a lot to start off with, and it's unlikely you'd want that much, but at least you have the option to expand if you want or need to. If you decide to sell on eBay instead of linking to your own website, the cost is US$37.99 per month. A yearly plan is US$287.99, a saving of about 40% on the monthly rate.

DHgate

This is a *huge* Chinese company that has worldwide factories dedicated to getting products to your customers. Its motto is Buy Globally, Sell Globally, and its range includes wedding gowns, phones and tablets, high-grade hair extensions, designer kids' clothing, home decor, to name a few.

BrandsDistribution

BrandsDistribution has been around since 2006, so it has stood the test of time. If you're interested in fashion dropshipping, this is the supplier for you. It has over 500,000 products from 120 fashion brands ready to be delivered, and it is free to subscribe to its newsletter. They offer drop-shipping with big discounts off the retail price with high-quality fashion brands such as Michael Kors, Versace, Gucci, Burberry, Adidas, Pierre Cardin, Laura Biagiotti, New Balance and Armani.

Oberlo

Oberlo is a subsidiary of Shopify, which allows you to dropship products directly from AliExpress and many other suppliers. It's a great application that allows you to find products, market them, and sell them on your own dropshipping website.

BelleWholesale

BelleWholesale is a business-to-business platform where brands, retailers and individual buyers can purchase up-to-the-minute women's apparel, shoes and accessories that are trending worldwide.

Women's fashion dropshippers

Women's fashion is obviously a hugely popular area for online shopping. When you go to many of these websites, not all of them will show information about dropshipping, so send them a message via their contact page.

Daring Diva Australia	This has great plus-size women's clothing from sizes 14–28, and also stocks a range of shoes, handbags and jewellery, all sourced from the USA and the UK.
Catch	You can use Catch as a dropship supplier, using its huge website and products as a drawcard to market your own products. Simply advertise their products (with a mark-up, of course), then once someone has made a purchase from your website, you log in to Catch, purchase that product, and then get it addressed to the person you sold it to and pocket the difference. Nifty, huh?
Modlily	This is an online fashion boutique that stocks inexpensive women's clothing, swimwear, plus-size fashion and jewellery, and offers free shipping on orders over US$69. If you become a fashion blogger or Instagram influencer you can join Modlily's Pro Program and get free fashion in exchange for promotion.
AliExpress	This is based in China but dropships worldwide. The products are very inexpensive, so make sure you get samples first to ensure the quality is what you expect. My tip: when looking for products such as women's fashion, ensure you tick the box that says 'Four stars and up' to ensure you get the most reputable supplier. Also, check how many orders each mini-seller has made – the higher the number, the more reputable they are.
Pink Queen	This is a China-based dropshipper that stocks women's lingerie, clothing, clubwear and accessories.

CC Wholesale Clothing	This manufactures women's apparel, plus-size fashion, jewellery, beauty items and shoes in the USA and dropships them around the world.
Arkhe Lane Activewear and Neyku Swimwear	These are sister companies based in Australia that offer dropshipping for women's swimwear. Contact them for information.

Custom T-shirt on-demand dropshippers

Have you ever fantasised about being a super successful T-shirt designer? I know I have. This fantasy can become a reality, since the technology is available for anyone to design their own T-shirt masterpiece and have it dropshipped directly to your customer. Check out these suppliers.

Dropshirt	This makes it easy for anyone to to sell customised T-shirts from any website – dropshipped straight to your customer. The dropship platform can be integrated with shopping carts such as Shopify, WooCommerce and Magento, perfect for your new e-commerce website.
The Print Bar	This company is based in Brisbane and allows you to sell T-shirts and other merchandise without any upfront expenses or storage needs. Also available are tea towels, drink bottles, lanyards, notebooks, pens, umbrellas, badges and USB sticks.
Tee Junction	This is a platform that allows you to design your T-shirt and open a simple store, and they print and send your orders on demand. You get a 20% commission on all sales. Tee Junction has T-shirts for men, women and children. Organic and free-trade T-shirts are available.
The Tshirt Mill	This company prints men's, women's and kids' T-shirts, accessories and homewares on demand and sends them directly to your customers. You just upload your design and you're ready to go!

8.8 Wholesale suppliers

Buying products at wholesale prices and then adding your retail mark-up when you sell to customers is one of the most traditional ways of doing business. It is tried and tested and has stood the passing of time. Of course, to get the best possible mark-up (and therefore profit), you need to make sure you are sourcing quality products for the best possible price.

Looking at price alone could leave you with poor-quality products and your customers won't come back if they receive a dodgy item. To get you on the right track, here are some wholesale suppliers that I've looked into across a variety of different products.

Eco and vegan clothing

If you're thinking about starting your own line of fashion, perhaps you could specialise in eco or vegan clothing. Creating fashion that is slow, friendlier for the environment, and produced ethically is highly valued by people who really care about where and how their clothing comes into being. Here are my favourite eco and vegan clothing wholesalers.

Donnah Clothing	This company is an organic fashion label designed in Australia. They create stylish clothing using natural/sustainable fibres while adhering to fair trade practices.
Global Sources	These are vegan-friendly clothing manufacturers and suppliers based in China with shipping all over the world.
My Heart Beats Green	This is an Australian brand offering organic cotton clothing, baby clothing and T-shirt printing.
NIOVI	This manufactures organic cotton baby clothing to specifications.
OCC Apparel	This offers high-quality Australian-made fabric knitted from certified organic cotton.

Soul Flower	This offers wholesale eco-friendly clothing for women, men, babies and kids.
Vegan Style	This is located in Fitzroy, Melbourne, and is a wholesaler of cruelty-free, fairly made, ecologically responsible clothing and shoes.
Velvety	This offers ethical fashion and vegan cosmetics.
Witjuti	This offers unique, eco-conscious bamboo clothing.

Adult products

Think of this as my 'sealed section'. Not a day goes by without people asking me what products they can sell online to make money right now, and my answer is always adult products! This is because adult products have a huge mark-up (anywhere between 30% and 300%, depending on where you are buying them), so there's a great opportunity to make a profit, and people often want to buy these products online because it's more discreet.

If you're planning on importing your products from overseas, you can afford to mark up the price 50–150%, probably even more if you can import them from China. If you're buying in bulk from Australia, you can really only mark up the cost around 30% if you want to stay competitive. Luxe products can be marked up more than low-cost products.

Hot tip: If you decide to go into this area, make sure you always find a way to package adult products discreetly if they are to be mailed or shipped. The reason adult products go so well online is because they can remain anonymous – so ensure packaging is plain and you choose a discreet business name to save embarrassment.

Here is a select list of where to find adult products at wholesale prices, including some that do dropshipping (see section 8.7).

AliExpress	This company has so many products, most of which are inexpensive, including a large range of adult products. I recommend buying from Sexy Love U Store, Secret Lover Store and Luvkis Official Store.
Xsales Adult Wholesaler	Based in NSW, this company offers bondage gear, fetish wear and an array of adult products. They don't offer a whole lot of information about how their wholesale and dropshipping works on their website – but we suggest you contact them direct.
Adult Wholesale Direct	This is based in the USA and carries well-known brands such as Doc Johnson, Trojan, Durex and Wet, with 65,000 products to choose from. Dropshipping adds a 5% surcharge to the price (which is extremely reasonable!).
Lifestyle Distributing	This is a wholesale distribution company based in the USA and carries loads of unique brands. There are no additional fees for dropshipping, and no minimum order requirements.

Baby and kids' fashion

This is a hugely popular area for online shopping and if you're buying wholesale rather than only offering dropshipping, you can also sell the products at markets. Check out some of these companies.

Blue Sky Kids Land	This company sells babywear, shoes, boys' and girls' clothing and formal wear at wholesale prices.
Candy Stripes Australia	This is a manufacturer, wholesaler and importer of top-quality garments for children and babies, with a fantastic range available.
Purebaby (Organic)	This company offers beautifully organic cotton baby clothes for newborn to four years at wholesale prices.
Designer Kidz	This is your one-stop wholesaler for gorgeous girls', boys' and babies' fashion. It is proudly Australian owned and operated for more than 25 years.

The Gibson Agency	They represent manufacturers to independent retailers across Queensland, Northern New South Wales and Northern Territory.

Bridal wholesalers

As already mentioned, weddings are big business and there is potential for huge profit in this area, though the price point for individual items is likely to be higher than many of the other areas I've looked at so far. Here are some companies to consider.

Annette of Melbourne Couture	This company has been making beautiful custom-made gowns for over 35 years, based in Seddon.
Cizzy Bridal Australia	A Perth-based family-owned business that supplies wholesale wedding gowns worldwide.
Cupid's Bridal Wholesale	Australian and internationally designed wedding gowns. Based in Perth.
Fiona Mary Warmbath Designs	This is based in Springwood, New South Wales.

Wholesale suppliers for essential oils

Whether you want to sell essential oils direct or make your very own cleaning or aromatherapy products, sourcing essential oils at a wholesale price is the first step. Here are some companies to look at.

ECO Modern Essentials	This is a Gold Coast-based company that specialises in Australian-certified organic pure oils and blends.
Ahimsa Oils	This has a vast selection of essential oil blends that can be used for aromatherapy and medicinal purposes. They offer organic, 100% pure and natural essential oils.

Amrita Aromatherapy	This company is based in the USA, but ships worldwide. You can order at a wholesale rate by providing your ABN number and purchasing a minimum of US$100 worth of products.
Aussie Soap Supplies	This company has been operating for 25 years.
Australian Wholesale Oils	This offers free shipping Australia-wide for orders over $200.

Jewellery wholesalers

Jewellery has always been a great product to sell online as it has a large price mark-up, making it quite profitable. My list covers fine jewellery wholesalers through to low-cost wholesalers of faux diamonds and costume jewellery.

Mignon and Mignon	This offers handmade jewellery inspired by special moments – it lives by the motto 'Cherish the simple things'. Its purpose is to provide a memento that will make someone remember meaningful moments in their life. Its products range from minimalist, versatile, for everyday wear, classic and chic.
Sunvsmoon	This offers minimalist boho handmade jewellery that's very affordable – the cheapest items cost AU$5. It's Adelaide-based and was established in 2014.
Crystal Eclipse Crowns	They are stockists of quartz-based products. While there are ready-made products available, it's well known for offering a made-to-order service. Everything is handcrafted and can be customised, making each product unique.
Nihao Jewelry	This is located in China, providing a one-stop shop for wholesale jewellery with no minimum order requirements and fast delivery all over the globe.

| Lady Rose Vintage Jewels | This is the place to go for vintage jewellery. Products are quite expensive for wholesaling, with prices ranging from AU$200 to over AU$6000, but are elegant and of good quality if this resonates with your place in the market. |

Wholesale lingerie sellers

The lingerie industry is booming! It's a fabulous choice for an online business model. For most small lingerie businesses, you need to either offer a wide range of choices that will suit a variety of body types or pick a niche to specialise in, such as:

- Plus-size lingerie
- Cosplay
- Latex lingerie
- Leather lingerie
- Lingerie subscription boxes

To help you along, here's a select list of wholesale lingerie sellers that won't put a hole in your pocket.

Lingerie Mart	This has been in the business for over 22 years and distributes brands including Affinitas, Be Wicked, Dreamgirl and Sophie B.
Lavinia Lingerie Inc	This was established in 2002, and is a great source of comfortable-to-wear lingerie that can fit up to J cup. The colours, moreover, are fashion-friendly, and its product range also includes bridal/honeymoon lingerie and activewear.
Theone Apparel	This offers collections of lingerie that are 10–20% cheaper than its competitors. The product range is of good quality and includes bodysuits and corsets.
Pink Queen Apparel Inc	This is one of the most acclaimed online lingerie stores around. It offers an affordable broad range of lingerie and clothing aimed at women aged 18 to 35.

8.9 White labelling or private label products

White labelling is when you buy a white- or private-label product and put your own branding on it for sale. This is not to be confused with passing off someone else's product as your own by slapping your own branding on it; these are products specifically sold for this purpose. This is big in the United States, but it's still an emerging area in Australia. Even though it's new here, there are companies that do it, and it could be a good fit for your business.

The primary area I'm going to focus on is beauty products because it's the most established area of white labelling. If you would love to get into the beauty industry with your own line of skincare, cosmetics or hair care, you can't just make them in your backyard and bottle it. There are strict regulations about ingredients, storage, testing and so on – it all gets really complicated!

But don't despair. There are manufacturers of these products that have already done all that hard work for you and will sell you their products wholesale for branding and sale. Some private label companies will make up a product according to what you are looking for (for example, all vegan ingredients) while others have a huge range of pre-made products. You choose the bottles and branding, and you have your very own line – all tested, labelled and bottled.

Not only is this model great for start-ups, it's also fantastic for hairdressers or people already in the beauty industry who want to increase their own brand and marketing with their own line of products.

Here are some companies to check out.

Private Label Skincare	PLSC creates skincare products from organic ingredients derived from the outback, Queensland rainforest and eastern coast, and uses sustainable packaging.

White Label Cosmetics & Packaging	This offers Australian-made and cruelty-free products at low minimum quantities. Custom formulations are also available, as well as a range of skincare packaging, such as bottles, droppers and jars.
YOUR Natural Products	This is a Queensland-based contract manufacturing company that designs and manufactures high-quality formulations.
ACPharm Private Label Skincare	This is run by a beauty therapist and pharmacist based in Queensland. They provide a large range of pharmaceutical grade skincare products, with multiple packaging and label options, and low minimum order quantities.
Botany Essentials	This company is based in Victoria and supplies organic beauty care products as well as contract manufacturing.
Natural Choice Cosmetics	This company is based in NSW and supplies base products and raw materials if you're keen to make your own line of skincare. The products are organic, and ethically and environmentally friendly.
Nature's Land Products	This company offers white label skincare manufactured in Melbourne, ranging from botanical-based formulas to high-tech cosmeceuticals.
Neon Cosmetics	This Melbourne-based company specialises in formulating and contract-manufacturing colour cosmetics.
Trulux	This company is based in Sydney; as well as manufacturing beauty products, it also handles product development, fulfilment, packaging, labels, photography and warehousing.
Machiaj Laboratories	This is a Victorian manufacturer of white label tanning and skincare products.
Vanilla Sugar	This Melbourne-based company can work with you on the design, manufacture and supply of private label products for your brand.

Hot tip: For a list of International White Label Cosmetic Suppliers, visit https://bit.ly/EAHMwhite

Conclusion

We covered a lot of ground in this chapter, from setting up your own website, including e-commerce functionality, and choosing a third-party platform to sell through. We also looked at the wonderful world of importing supplies and products for sale, including the efficient new model of dropshipping, with comprehensive lists of sources for a broad range of business types. The whole world really is your oyster with options like these. Check out some of these companies for inspiration and see how easy it can be to get started!

Chapter 9

Marketing your business

So you've made your business plan, chosen your product, launched your business . . . and then you remembered that these are just your first steps as an entrepreneur. The next job is to market your business to get sales. Marketing is a pivotal component of any business. You must think of innovative ways to get your brand and product noticed so that you can attract customers.

In this chapter, we'll look at all the options for marketing your business. It's not just about a pretty ad in a print medium anymore – there are so many more ways to promote your brand. Because I have marketing whiz Nicole Millard on my team, I've asked her to create this chapter. She's going to show you how you can maximise free and paid advertising and marketing avenues to reach larger audiences. Over to you, Nic!

9.1 Why marketing is important

Marketing is an indispensable stage of your business journey. People must know you exist before they can buy from you, and the more people who buy from you, the more popular your brand will become.

Word of mouth is the best way to get buyers talking about your offering. This organic hyping is more effective than spending thousands of dollars on advertising, so you need to be strategic in your marketing efforts. A website is the first step, which we've covered extensively in Chapter 8, but another way to get that buzz started is to sell offline as well as through your website; for example, by booking stalls at trade fairs, markets or pop-up shops, and at any other event that will help promote your brand and business. This is a great way to get some customers for initial reviews and get that word of mouth started! It lets people see the product in real life so they can test the quality first and then they might become more comfortable purchasing later online.

If you're serious about your business, but it isn't growing as you hoped, and you aren't sure where you went wrong or even how to best devote your energies to it, it might be worth hiring a business coach. These guys are experts in everything business, and no matter what your niche, they can provide really useful information and advice about launching and creating a successful business. Business coaches can be found locally or online, and they're worth every penny!

Social media is such a huge part of our lives, it definitely should form the basis of your business marketing strategy – that's why the rest of this chapter is all about social media. However, here are some other market-ing ideas to consider adding to round everything out and cover more ground:

- Add your business to 'google my business'.
- Use email marketing.
- Set up a customer loyalty program or a referral program where a customer gets some kind of discount or freebie if they refer others to you.
- Attend networking and industry events.
- Nominate your business for local business awards.
- Host local events or workshops.
- Join your local chamber of commerce.
- Collaborate with other businesses for cross promotions.
- Send your product to an influencer for promotion.
- Hand out business cards or pamphlets.

- Advertise via print media, local billboards, radio or TV.
- Sponsor a sports team.
- Produce car decals with your business logo and contact details and give them to friends and family.
- Become an event speaker.
- Give out free products or service samples.
- Be involved in fundraising or charity.

9.2 Social media marketing

When starting a new business, lots of people wonder whether they actually need to be on social media at all. My answer? HECK YES!

We've talked about this a bit already, but social media is really the best place to start promoting your brand, starting with your friends and family, who can share to their friends and so on. Even with your own website, you'll still need social media to drive people to your website, and for word of mouth publicity.

Social media communities can make or break any business in this day and age, so even before you launch your brand, start to talk about your business and gather as many followers as possible before your official launch. Give your business a human face and take suggestions directly from prospective buyers. An engaged audience will be priceless in growing your business.

Social media is the cheapest form of advertising you'll ever use for your business and it's here to stay for a long time, so the best thing to do is embrace it and learn how to make it work best for you. I'm going to run through some of my best hints and tricks to using social media for your business. I have been using social media for about ten years, and managing social media has been my career for about nine of those years, so I've picked up quite a lot over that time. I am mostly self-taught, and much of what I have learned about social media has been through trial and error. I've made every mistake under the sun and discovered lots of little secrets along the way. So, you'll get the benefit of all I have stored in my brain, and you can even consider it a shortcut to success (it gives me warm fuzzies to know that I can pass on the knowledge I have learned to help you).

Now, there are loads of different social media platforms, and if you're new to the social media game, the choice can be overwhelming. One thing I will say to you now: your business does NOT need to be on every single social media platform!

Okay, I hear you breathe a massive sigh of relief.

What I tell my clients is that, as a rule of thumb, your business really only needs to be on one or two platforms – three at the very most. My suggestion is to choose one primary platform to be present on, and then one or two others where you share your content too. This will stop you from becoming overwhelmed and overloaded. Look at your target demographic, and figure out which social media they will most likely be engaging on, and go from there. For example, Stay At Home Mum's main platform is Facebook. This is because our leading demographic of Australian females, aged 25–45, who are parents and the main grocery shopper in the household, are regular Facebook users. Our other two platforms on which we have a large audience are Instagram and Pinterest, for much the same reasons as Facebook.

Let's run through some of the more prominent social media platforms you may be using as a business, and weigh up the pros and cons of each.

Facebook

Facebook is still one of the most widely used social media platforms even though it's been around for so long. Mind you, Instagram is hot on its heels, especially for business owners. Facebook should definitely be a part of the brand awareness and advertising strategy for any business. The platform itself is free to use – its paid advertising component is purely optional. You can, if you wish, use Facebook to market your business effectively, and still use it for free.

Facebook is a great way for businesses to get their brand out there to the masses – you have lots of different options for how your business page looks, options such as shops and appointment calendars, you can display the services you offer and allow your customers (and potential customers) to contact you. If there is one social media platform to be on, this is it!

Pros:

- It's essentially free to use.
- Most people still have a Facebook account, so you have a wide target audience.
- Facebook ads are cheaper than advertising the old-school way such as print, radio and TV.

Cons:

- Facebook changes the goalposts constantly so you need to keep up with that to get the most out of it.
- There is no easy way to contact Facebook customer service, so if you have any problems with the platform, you are often left to work it all out on your own.

Instagram

Instagram used to be seen as just for the 'beautiful people' of the celebrity world to hang out, mainly because of its concentration on imagery and the younger demographic that used the platform. Once Facebook took over the reins in 2012, Instagram has become a powerful marketing tool for many businesses. Some industries will perform better on Instagram than others – these are usually those with visually appealing content, such as food-related businesses, hair and beauty businesses, fashion businesses, wedding-related businesses, photographers and the like.

Like Facebook, Instagram allows you to sell products from posts, plus it has a business page option so you can add your contact details. Instagram also has an offshoot called IGTV – this is where you can post long-form videos (over 1 minute), which can be previewed on your Instagram feed. You can also pay to promote your posts on Instagram.

Pros:

- It's a lot of fun and can showcase your business in a creative way.
- You can cross-promote your posts on your Facebook business page if they are linked.

Cons:

- If the nature of your business means it isn't visually appealing, it can be difficult to get a following.

Pinterest

Pinterest is an interesting platform because it's not quite social media, yet not quite a search engine either – it's more like a cross between both. This platform has been around since 2010 and has become one of the most influential platforms for businesses. Aimed mostly at women, Pinterest is a place where people share their favourite things, from fashion and jewellery, to hairstyles, beauty tips and home decor ideas. It's like a massive vision board.

Businesses can capitalise on the demographic by 'pinning' their products to boards that are seen by millions of people everyday. It can be a great platform to get your business noticed. You can pay to promote your pins on Pinterest for that added amplification.

Pros:

- You can get loads of ideas for products and your business in general from other 'pinners'.
- It can be great for getting traffic to your website, and therefore sales.

Cons:

- Pinterest is definitely more widely used in the USA than it is in Australia, so it may be more difficult to sell to an Australian audience.

Twitter

Twitter is widely used by major brands, big businesses and celebrities and can be a very loud and busy place. Depending on your target demographic, it can be quite a useful business tool to promote brand awareness and conversation around your product or service. Twitter has a paid ad option that you can use for amplification.

Pros:

- You can join in conversations ('tweets') with brands and celebrities and hopefully get noticed.

Cons:

- There can be lots of nastiness and negativity with a high presence of trolls on Twitter, which could be detrimental to your brand.

LinkedIn

LinkedIn is a social media network that concentrates mostly on business relationships, networking and career development. You can connect with like-minded people in your business industry, and also share your own business achievements and goals with others. There is a paid ad option in LinkedIn to promote your posts, and you can also join groups.

Pros:

- You can meet like-minded people in your industry and form some valuable business connections.
- You can learn a lot in general about business.

Cons:

- It can be a tad boring and a lot of what is in your newsfeed may not be relevant to you.
- You may be randomly contacted by other businesses or people who want to sell to you.

YouTube

YouTube is a video sharing platform that has been around since 2005. Users can upload their own video content, subscribe to channels and share video content to other places on the internet. Many businesses use YouTube to host their videos, which can be followed by anyone in the world, so it can be a great marketing tool. Like Facebook, YouTube has a very broad demographic, so can be used to reach people of all ages if you have a business that lends itself to great video material. You can also pay to advertise on the YouTube platform.

Pros:

- You can post short and long form videos to a wide demographic.
- It's free to use.

Cons:

- It can be time-consuming to upload the videos and caption them.
- It has much slower growth than other platforms.

Snapchat

Snapchat is a great social media platform to go for if you are targeting a young demographic with your products or services. It is basically a messaging app where messages and images disappear after they are viewed. Many businesses and brands have mastered the art of appealing to the younger generation on Snapchat with upbeat, fun imagery and videos. You can create a business account and also use its paid advertising portal.

Pros:

- It is widely used by teens and young adults, so is the perfect place for your business-to-be if that is your target audience.
- It's lots of fun!

Cons:

- It can be really tricky if you don't know how to use it well. You have to be on the app constantly and consistently to gain an audience, which can be difficult if you are running a business.

TikTok

TikTok is one of the newer kids on the social media block. It is a Chinese-developed video app that became massively popular in 2018 when it merged with another similar app called Musical.ly. Like Snapchat, it is aimed at a young demographic of teens to young adults, and is the most popular social media platform today in this genre. TikTok can be used for business, especially if you have a knack for creating videos. Influencer marketing is huge there at the moment, so it's worth trying if you are targeting a younger age group. There is also a paid ad option for businesses.

Pros:

- It's new and it's fun.
- You can be creative and get yourself noticed pretty quickly.

Cons:

- Most users are quite young (though this may change), so if your target audience is older, TikTok might not be the best platform for you.

But what do you post?

This is a common question I get asked by business owners, and the answer, unfortunately, is 'How long is a piece of string?' It really depends on the type of business you have and also what social media platform you're on as to what you will post. My best recommendation is to look at as many other businesses' posts as you can on the platform you've chosen for inspiration, and then put your own spin on it. For example, people love to see behind the scenes. So images of you making the product or packing the product can go a long way towards building trust. Here are a few suggestions of what types of things you might want to post and which platforms they will work best on.

Video content

At the moment, most platforms favour video posts; that is, they prioritise showing these in feeds over static posts (photos). Facebook, Instagram, Twitter, LinkedIn, Snapchat and, of course, YouTube and TikTok, all encourage their users to post video content.

Most businesses can use video easily and effectively in their social media marketing, but many people are a little unsure how to do it, or are just plain scared! Here are a few tips that might help:

- You can use your mobile phone! Your videos don't have to be an epic production with lighting, make-up, sound gear and all the bells and whistles. Sure, it would look amazing if you had all of those things, but you want to do this as cheaply as you can when you're getting started, especially if you decide to do a lot of video posts.

- Upload your videos directly to your account rather than only uploading to one and then sharing it on other platforms. This will help it get higher reach, engagement and views.

- Make sure you get your main message out to the viewer within the first 10 to 15 seconds. That will determine whether they stay to watch the video or turn it off.

- Make sure your thumbnail is eye-catching and high quality – and not some shot of you with your mouth hanging open mid-sentence. Some social platforms will auto-generate a thumbnail when you upload a video, but you can change it and add your own.

- Ensure that you always write a caption and heading to go with your video – it will catch more eyes in a newsfeed and make people stop scrolling if they know what the video is about.

- Use different types of videos – you don't always have to upload the same type. You can use a mix of live, tutorials, informational, behind the scenes and Q&A formats.

- Build some buzz around your new videos, especially if you're making an announcement or launching a new product or service. Tell people a day, or even a few hours, before you post it that it'll be coming up.

- Over 85% of Facebook users watch videos with the sound off, so when posting a video, use a captioning tool whenever possible – and make sure you edit it. You can also make it clear in your post whether the viewer needs their sound turned on to get the most out of the video.

- If you have a blog on your website, you can embed your videos into the blog post on your website. That will definitely help increase views.

- Try to be yourself, make your audience laugh, and don't worry if you make a mistake or if it's not perfect. Consumers love realness and authenticity. The less perfect it is, the better!

If you're not too comfortable in front of the camera, that's okay! You can still make slideshow videos that will rank in the social media newsfeeds quite well. Facebook has its own slideshow option, in which you can add images and also choose from a small list of music tracks to add. It's quick and easy and looks really effective.

There's also online video making software available that you can use to make amazing-looking videos – some of these have free versions (but this usually will include some sort of proprietary watermark). I think it can be worth paying for the pro versions if you're going to be creating lots of videos, as there are fewer restrictions and they look more professional.

Here are some of my favourite video creation websites for you to have a look at:

- Animoto
- Wave.video
- Adobe Spark
- Wrapr
- Clipchamp
- Ripl

Using images to tell your story

The types of images you can post are endless – there are memes, static images, GIFs, or if your phone has these more advanced options, even panoramic images, 360 images and 3D images.

Memes (usually a combination of images and words that are clever or humorous, made for sharing) are really popular on Facebook and always generate high engagement and reach because of their 'shareability'. You can create your own using Photoshop or websites such as Canva, or you can share memes made by other people that relate to your business.

A static image is just a beautifully shot photograph. You can upload your own photos to your Facebook page, or you can obtain stock photos. Stock photos are professional photographs of common places, landmarks, nature, events or people that are licensed for use by others, including commercially (that's you!). You can license and download stock images from many places on the internet. There are free sites such as Pexels and Unsplash – if you use images from sites like these, you usually only need to credit the person who originally uploaded the image when you post it. Otherwise you can join a subscription or credit-based stock image site such as Bigstock, Shutterstock, iStock, Fotolia and Alamy, where you pay to use professional photos either per image or through a subscription model.

A GIF (Graphics Interchange Format) is a series of images (or soundless video) that loops continuously. They have been growing in popularity over the last few years and are a fun way of generating some engagement on your social accounts. You can post them either in the comments of a post, or you can post them directly as you would an image or video. If you directly upload a GIF on Facebook it will post as a video, so you'll need to add a heading and so on. You can make your own GIF on a website called Giphy, or there's lots of other sites you can use too if you do a search. You can also make basic GIF animations in the Pro version of Canva.

Here are a few useful tips for posting any of these types of image on social media:

- Make sure you always use high-resolution images; otherwise they'll look small and fuzzy. Check how they look on a phone, tablet and laptop or desktop computer to make sure they look good.
- All social media platforms have recommended dimensions for images, so it's a good idea to familiarise yourself with these – and they change all the time. There are several websites you can go to to check on the dimensions (I like Louise M as she has an update at the beginning of every year). Otherwise I just use Canva for my images because it has the correct-sized templates!
- Repurpose your content and images. Just because you have already posted an image, that doesn't mean you can't reuse it on another platform or later down the track. This will help to make sure you always have good content on your page, plus it saves time.
- If you make your own memes, add your logo or website to the image. If people share that image, then your branding goes with it.
- Tell a story with your meme/image – always write a caption to go with it. Ask a question, say something funny or tell a story to get people commenting and sharing.

- You don't have to always directly upload imagery – have a look for some relatable content from other pages that you can share directly to your own socials. This can save time, but always credit and tag the original poster's social media account. Better still, flick them a private message and ask them if you can use their image first.
- Make yourself familiar with the community standards and policies of the social media platforms you use before you post (this goes for videos too). Nobody wants to get blocked for sharing or posting an image that breaches standards.
- Always post imagery that is relevant to your business and your customers. You want your branding and tone to be as consistent as possible so people recognise your content. That said, try to keep things fresh.
- Take note of what sorts of images work best and resonate well with your followers – and keep doing more of that.
- One word of advice I will give you that is hugely important – do not just go to Google Images and steal other people's photos. Just because they are there does not mean they are free for you to use as your own. If you do this, you risk being sued and paying for breaching copyright.

Using links on social media

Posting links to your website on your social media accounts is a great way to start building traffic to your site. Although the reach and engagement of your post may not be as high as if you posted a video or image, it'll still get some traction, especially if your content is awesome. If you don't have your own website or blog, you can easily post links to websites and blogs with great information that supports your own business.

Just note that it's a little trickier to post links onto platforms such as Instagram or TikTok, but you can use the link in your profile bio on these accounts to drive traffic.

Here's some useful tips for getting engagement when posting links on your social media accounts:

- Try asking a question when posting a link. Posting a link itself may not get much engagement, unless you ask your audience a question.

- Don't use 'clickbait' headings. Clickbait is when you use attention-grabbing headlines to lure readers into clicking on normally uninteresting content; for example, 'You won't believe what happened to this woman!' It's very unattractive to most users, meaning your engagement will tank, and this practice will de-rank your post, so your reach will also go down the toilet.
- Ensure that the link preview has a good-quality image – this is difficult if the link comes from a website you don't own, but sometimes you can change the image within the social media platform itself.
- Make sure the information in the link is relevant to your business and customers and encourage readers to click on the link with a call to action.
- Check the link and always read through the information to make sure you are not posting an inactive link or anything spammy.

If you're not sure what copy to write on the post with the link, have a read through the article itself and grab a quote or meaningful phrase and use that as your intro. That way you don't have to think about what to say, because the hard work has already been done.

Cheap or free ways to market your business on social media

There are plenty of options available for you to boost posts and engage people outside your usual circle of followers by paying for advertising, but there are also heaps of cheap and free ways to effectively market. Here are a few ideas:

- Ask your friends and family to follow or like your social media accounts (but don't be too pushy about it).
- Talk to your audience, share what you have been up to with your product – let them enjoy the journey with you.
- Ask your customers to leave a review or feedback.
- Triple check that your contact details are correct on your social media platforms. You would be surprised how many people leave up old numbers or inactive websites.

- Join online business groups in your area to network.
- Do regular live videos. People love watching videos and they love to see the real you.
- Share the content of larger social media accounts – and credit them. It's a good way to get noticed.
- Engage on other social media business accounts as your own business by commenting and liking posts that are about topics similar to your own product or service. People will start to notice you and click through to your own account – and they might even follow you!
- Offer to do guest articles for other websites on your products or services.
- Add a blog to your website and post about it on your accounts.
- Load all your videos onto YouTube and then link them to your other social media accounts. If you get enough views you can even start monetising your channel and be paid by YouTube.
- Offer people something for free in exchange for signing up to your email list, such as a free ebook or digital download.
- Ask other businesses to be a guest contributor on your social media accounts.
- Create a supporting Facebook group for your Facebook page – and keep it exclusive to customers.
- Always have a 'call to action' on posts. Click Here, Join Now, Grab Your Copy, etc.

9.3 How to talk to your audience

Social media is called what it is for a reason. It's social! Over the years I have seen many businesses come and go on social media, and one thing that I guarantee will make a business one of the 'stayers' is to talk to its audience regularly and in a way that is engaging. That is the best way to build a strong and loyal following.

Too many times, I have spoken to business owners who say, 'I have a Facebook page, but I can't get anyone to follow it or talk on it, so

I'm just giving up! It doesn't work.' When I ask them how often they post and what they post on their page, a common answer is, 'Oh I post now and then, maybe once a month if I think of it. And I just post a meme or tell them my opening times or something. I dunno.' That, in a nutshell, is why that business is not succeeding on social media. Here are my top tips for a successful social media presence for your business.

Post on social media regularly

By regularly, I mean more than every now and then when you think of it. You must decide how often you'll post on each platform, and stick to it as much as possible so that people remember you and, possibly even more important, the algorithm remembers you! It doesn't have to be five times a day, don't worry. If you can aim to post at least twice per week on each platform, that's plenty. I personally wouldn't post any less than once per week per account.

Post consistently

By consistently, I mean post on the same days of the week, at the same times. Think hard about your target demographic and when they are most likely to be online. For example, Stay At Home Mum targets mums, of course. So we like to concentrate on putting up our best posts every day in the evenings between 6 and 10pm, as that's the time when our audience is most likely to have sorted dinner, put the kids to bed and be sitting down in front of the TV – which is when most people scroll through their Facebook feed.

You can use tools such as Buffer or Hootsuite to schedule your content in a consistent manner so you don't have to remember to do it on time. Or alternatively, just use the scheduling tools on your social media accounts themselves if they have them – it's better as it's free and easy to use. These tools also mean you can queue up a number of posts when you have time, and then dole them out over the next week. Just make sure you don't schedule too far in advance in case your post becomes out of date or inappropriate; for example, it might look insensitive to your followers if you post something silly when a tragic event has just happened in your city.

Be conversational in your posts

I always think the best posts on any social media platform are the ones that make me feel like the writer of that post is talking directly to me. Like we're having a chat at the school gate. My eyes glaze over if I see a post that has no personality behind it. So be conversational, and most of all, be yourself!

Ask questions

Nothing gets conversation flowing more than when you engage your followers with questions. You'll get more out of open-ended questions rather than straight yes/no ones. For example, you might have two product ideas but you're not sure which one would sell better, so ask your audience! It's like free market research right there! And it'll get your engagement up if you ask in the right way. Instagram lets you do polls in its story function, or you can post two photos side by side and ask what people think.

Answer questions or just have a chat

If your followers ask a question in post comments or in messages, for the love of all that is good, please answer them! There's nothing worse than being ignored. They can and will go find someone else to buy from if they don't get an answer from you in a decent timeframe. Now, I'm not saying you need to be glued to your social media all day every day (I mean, you have a business to run, right?), but check your notifications at the very least once a day to make sure you aren't missing anything, especially in the hours after you know you've scheduled a post.

If you have a few minutes to spare, hop onto Facebook or Instagram or whatever your favourite platform is, and have a chat to your followers in the comments. Even if it's just saying thanks, or acknowledging their comment, they will love it. This is a great way to build loyalty and trust.

9.4 How to deal with trolls, negative comments and reviews, and scammers

Ahh, the internet. It can be such a lovely place full of positivity and creativity and inspiration, but it can also be a cesspool where people stoop to the lowest of behaviour because of the anonymity that the internet affords them. Sometimes it's simply annoying and sometimes it's genuinely harmful to your business – or even illegal in the case of scammers. Let's look at some of the specifics of what you might encounter and what to do about it.

Trolls

Trolls are unfortunately something nearly all people face when running a social media account for their business – and it can be a soul-destroying experience! The reasons they do it are varied. Sometimes it's a complete stranger who has taken it upon themselves to be nasty. But often (and unfortunately), it's somebody you know or a competitor. From experience, I can say that the first two years of running a social media account for your business will truly be the worst when it comes to dealing with trolls. And it is your job to weed them all out – but we'll get to that. Here are some tips for dealing with trolls.

Have a policy on behaviour on your social media platforms

Spell out everything that you *don't* want on your page; for example, some pages make it clear that racist or homophobic comments will result in being banned, or they might ban users from advertising their own work. Encourage people to read your rules before commenting – even though most people won't bother, it's worth a shot. That way, if it comes to truly bad behaviour, you can point people towards the rules they've broken, and delete and ban them.

Identify the trolls - delete and ban

All true trolls should be deleted and banned from your business social media accounts. No contact, no reply. That's what they want – to engage you – so don't give them the satisfaction. After having your accounts for a while, you will be able to spot trolls a mile away – and you may even delight in the deleting and banning process.

If you aren't sure whether they are actually trolling, give them one chance – and one chance only. Ask them publicly (and very nicely) to refer to your rules. A true follower will apologise and stick to the rules. However, a troll will start up the negative behaviour again, send you messages or stir up trouble on your page. So, delete and ban.

What happens if you receive a scathing email after deleting and banning? Again, they are just trying to engage you in a fight – and anything you say will probably be screenshotted and shared. So don't engage. Put all emails of this nature into a separate folder to ignore, but don't delete them in case you need to refer to it in future.

'Feed them to the wolves'

Okay, this tactic is for large social accounts that have a really passionate following. If a troll starts something on your page, leave it there – and wait. Your followers will defend you to the ends of the earth, without you having to do a thing! Of course, don't make a habit of this, but seeing it occasionally will not only make you look good, but will empower your fans too!

Keep a close eye on things, though; this sort of behaviour should always be moderated in case the troll starts giving your fans too much trouble. In that case, delete and ban, and then send the fans that defended you a message thanking them for doing so.

Some trolls we've had over the years

'You club baby seals.'

About six months into the start of the Stay at Home Mum Facebook page, our brand-new website had just gone online. One of the very first articles on the website was 'How to Make Your Own Homemade Baby Wipes' – and it's still there! Anyway, a troll got onto the Facebook page and started going ballistic because not all of the ingredients were vegan and green. She began to call us and other users terrible names and would not stop. After we deleted and banned her, we received an email: 'If you use those ingredients to make homemade baby wipes, you may as well club baby seals.'

Jody printed out the email and put it up on the wall of her office for years because it made us chuckle. To be clear, she's entitled to her views about our products, but she was not entitled to abuse us and others for not sharing those views, and that's why we banned her.

'I hope your family die in a fire.'

This is probably the most terrible troll we've ever had. About six or seven years ago, another money-saving blogger messaged Jody to say we had copied content from one of her articles. Many, many money-saving bloggers cover very similar content, but we had not copied her work! We politely told her that, and confirmed that Jody writes all the articles herself. She didn't believe us, and unfortunately it escalated rather quickly, so we ended up blocking her messages on the site. Then she started calling the office around the clock and leaving messages on the answering machine. We got her number blocked. Then the bombardment of emails started.

When she emailed to say that she hoped that Jody and her family would all die in a fire – yes, really! – we referred the matter to the police. She was completely out of line! The best bit? When Jody looked at the content in question, it was an exact copy of an article that Jody had written three years earlier. Grr!

Negative reviews

Remember this: a true negative review is *not* trolling. If you receive a negative review on your Facebook page, Google Business page or other social media platform from a real customer about a true experience, you'll want to delete it instantly – but don't. Here's why: let your audience see how you handle the negativity. Reply to the negative reviewer's comment and ask them how you can fix the problem or do better next time, taking the time to really listen to their feedback.

Don't engage in a huge online screaming match – that is guaranteed to scare future customers away. If you handle the negative criticism the right way, people can see you genuinely wish to help your customers sort out any problems they may have. Be as humble and respectful as you possibly can. And if you can't come to a solution, explain to them (under their comment) exactly why you can't – without being mean or snarky. And then leave it at that – even if they keep going.

Scammers

Whether you have an online business or simply use the internet for email, shopping and banking, you will inevitably come across scammers. These dodgy people are seemingly everywhere, and they are getting more creative every day with their scams. So how do you know what's legit and what's bogus? I'll give you a few tips.

Email scammers

Never click on a link in an email unless you are expecting that email – it could be a phishing scam where someone is trying to get your personal login information to a trusted site; for example, I get fake PayPal emails all the time asking me to click a link and log in. On one of them, I looked very carefully at the email address and noticed that there was a number 1 instead of a letter 'l' in the PayPal web address, so it looked like this: Paypa1.com. So easy to overlook!

If it looks legit, but it is unexpected, go to their website and log in to your account yourself – not through the link – or find a phone number you can call to make sure the email is genuine.

Social media scammers

Social media scammers are a little easier to spot – they ask you to direct message (DM) them. Sure, there may be a legitimate reason to send a direct message, but never do a business transaction through a DM. Get them to email the information from their email address.

Phone calls are also a common method scammers use. Never ever say 'Yes' to anything over the phone. If someone calls you and it sounds interesting, have them email you so you can see where their email has come from. Unsolicited phone calls are often used by scammers as the first point of contact because it can be hard to say no to someone on the phone.

Never ever *ever* give any details over the phone about your address or bank account details.

Other ways to spot a scammer:

- They pressure you to make a decision on the spot.
- They can belittle you or make you feel emotional or embarrassed.
- Their email is full of spelling and grammatical mistakes.
- They won't answer any questions directly.
- They mention gift cards as a payment method.
- The name of their business is similar to a reputable business.
- Your gut says something isn't right . . . Listen to it!

Conclusion

Marketing is essential for getting your brand on the map and your product or service out there for people to start buying. As you've now seen, social media is the cheapest and easiest way to get started. You don't have to be a whiz at it to get some decent accounts set up and working for your business. Of course, you may well encounter the less-great side of the internet in the shape of trolls and scammers – but now you know how to handle those. Have fun with it, support other small brands (and they'll hopefully support you back) and you'll start seeing your customers find you!

Chapter 10

Blogging for a profit

A blog can take lots of forms, but usually it's an individual's website about their life or a specific topic with stories about what they've been up to, with accompanying photos. For example, a lot of bloggers write about travel, cooking, their families and their homes. Sometimes they're just for fun, but the really successful bloggers with a big following can make decent money from their blog through advertising, affiliate links (see Chapter 11) and even book deals and so on.

Chances are, you already know someone who has a blog. Starting your own site from scratch may seem like an awfully daunting notion – but it's really fun to have your very own piece of the internet! If you think about it, you never really own a Facebook page or Instagram account because of the nature of those platforms, but a website is an asset – *your* saleable asset. And the more work you put into it, the more articles you write and the more followers you accumulate, the more that website will be worth!

How much income can you really make blogging? Well, my answer is, how hard do you want to work? I have been blogging as my only source of income for ten years now. Yes, it is hard work; yes, I put an incredible amount of time into it. But I really enjoy it – I find it so much fun to wake up in the morning and think, 'What am I going to write about today?'

Successful bloggers all seem to have a few traits in common:

- They are often people who are easily bored. That is, normal work just doesn't hold their attention.
- They are do-ers.
- They go against the grain of what is considered 'normal'.
- They are tenacious – they don't give up.
- They ask questions. And no questions are ever silly.
- They are true to themselves.
- They love being told 'You can't do that!' and proving everyone wrong.

Great bloggers make money because they don't give up and they do what needs to be done. But just a word on money – I didn't take a wage for the first two years of running my blog. Every cent my blog made was re-invested into making the blog bigger and better, by adding features, making it more user-friendly and paying other writers to contribute to the content. This in turn made the blog more popular, so it made *more* money, and so the wheel goes round. So if you don't have a huge amount of cash to invest in your blog (and that's okay), the reality is that you have to put in the time and hard work instead, especially if you want your blog to become your full-time job.

You need a clear strategy for starting your blog and monetising it if you want to make money, and that's what this chapter is all about. Blogging is just like any other business out there. You get out of it what you put into it – including your time, your energy and your passion.

10.1 Find your blog niche

As mentioned, a lot of blogs are just about you, your lifestyle and what you're doing – a bit like a diary. These blogs are fun, but rarely profitable. On the other hand, having a *niche* blog on one particular topic – now, that's where the money is! Niche bloggers often become experts on their topics. A journalist or writer may seek a blogger's expertise for interviews; this will also help build an audience.

What do *you* want to blog about? Sometimes you will know before you start, other times you have to find your niche. Have a really thorough brainstorming session about what you write about consistently (and what you can monetise well). Writing about a topic that you're passionate about is a damn good start – your passion for your topic will show through and help you connect with followers. Is there a blog you follow but whose topic you think you could do a better job with? Checking out your potential competition is a great way to get ideas for what you like and what you don't.

Bloggers are often divided into two camps – the 'experts' in a particular field, and those 'learning along the way'. You don't need to be a expert if you write about your journey. In fact, the bumps along the way often make the best content as readers will relate to your story.

Some niche ideas include:

- A diary of your travels
- Business strategies
- Fishing, sport or dance
- Fashion for plus-size women
- Cooking, cleaning or parenting
- Real estate
- Dating and relationship advice
- Crafts, including sewing, knitting and crochet
- Health and wellness
- Weight loss
- Vegan living
- Ethically or sustainably sourced lifestyle

10.2 Choose a name

I often think that choosing a name for your blog is the hardest part! Just like choosing a business name, you need something that is descriptive but also unique and hasn't been used yet, so you can be found easily online and can acquire things like domain name and social media handles with that name. See Chapter 7 for lots more about choosing business names (your blog name, in this instance), and buying and registering domains.

I always like to make the suggestion of using your nickname or similar as it's what makes *you* special! But if you already have a business and want to add a blog to your repertoire, you may well already have a great concept and name that you can extend to your blog.

10.3 Choose a platform and build your blog

All websites – your blog in this instance – need a platform on which to be built. When I started Stay at Home Mum, I used Facebook to set up a page, and simply started posting every day. It was free and a great way to build a following. But after a few months, I realised I needed my own website. Then I used the Facebook page to let people know about it so they could read more there.

Hosting your blog

To get your blog on the internet, you need to find a host for your website. The place where you buy your domain name often offers hosting services, or you can choose your very own web hosting company. Not all hosting is alike. Some hosts are made for little blogs and are priced accordingly, while others are more expensive and cater to huge websites. Think about what you need now, but also what you might want to include on your site in the future; for example, can your blog handle a lot of videos, or only photos? Do you think you'll want an e-commerce store one day? You can often upgrade with the same host, so look into what a hosting service can offer if your blog becomes popular and you need to be able to accommodate a lot of traffic to your site, or if you want to expand it to include other features, such as additional functionality.

For reviews and services of each host, check out the reviews and comparison site, Aussie Hosting. It has an article called 'Best Web Hosting Australia: 2021 Reviews' that's updated all the time. It's an easy read, and it lists the pricing for all the hosts and the services offered by each.

There are both free platforms and paid platforms out there that you can use. Let's look at some of the options and why you might choose one over the other.

Free platforms

Free might sound too good to be true, and in my opinion these are a bit of a trap. When you have your blog on a free platform, your blog name will be something along the lines of 'MyBlog.Tumblr.com.au' and it really does scream 'I couldn't afford a self-hosted blogging account'. Which is all well and good if you're just doing it for fun. But it does look unprofessional. Also, you don't own your blog – the platform does. If you want to make money from your blog, it's important to remember (and this is a biggie) *you can't do paid advertising on a free platform*. Go back and read that sentence again. There is no functionality for it – and you aren't allowed to do it.

Free blogging platforms include:

- Wordpress.com
- Blogger
- Tumblr
- Wix

Paid platforms

Don't panic! Paid platforms aren't as expensive as you might think, and they offer a lot of benefits that you'll want if you're serious about making money from your blog. Most paid platforms in the blogging sphere are known as self-hosted blogs. You might be thinking, 'Why is it called self-hosted if I'm paying a third-party host?' but that's just how it works. You own it and are fully in charge, but you pay a small fee to keep it online. It also means you can sell it. Plus you can advertise to your heart's content – and advertising means money in the bank.

Self-hosted platforms include:

- WordPress.org (not to be confused with Wordpress.com)
- Shopify

- WooCommerce
- Squarespace
- Weebly (best for non-techie people)

One of the most popular platforms for blogs is WordPress.org (not to be confused with the free option that ends with .com), and that's what I use. I love it – it's free to get started, pretty user-friendly, scales up as you need it to, and has loads of plug-ins (that is, additional functionalities you can add to your website for free or small fee).

The cons of self-hosted platforms are:

- They are harder to set up than their free counterparts.
- You need to pay a hosting fee.
- If you get stuck or run into trouble, you will probably need to pay someone to help.

If you're a bit tech-savvy and are keen to go down the self-hosted path so that you can monetise your blog, now is the time to look into the different options and decide what you want.

First you need to know what you want your blog to do and what you want it to look like so. Your blog should be a reflection of you – your likes, your style. I highly suggest having a look around at blogs you really like, and writing down what you like about them. Is it the colour, how it works, the font, the style? It also has to be user-friendly and fast!

If you just want to write articles and monetise the site, I would go with WordPress. I like it because it offers themes (templates that determine how it functions and what it looks like) that you can customise. There are both free and paid themes available – of course, the paid themes have more functionality and features, and are generally prettier. Once you have a theme installed, it's pretty easy to drop in photographs and change the name. Have a good play with WordPress so you know how it all works and check out YouTube for tutorials – there are heaps! I always recommend starting simple, then building your way up.

If you want to have products for sale *and* a blog you can monetise, you may need both WordPress and an e-commerce platform such as

Shopify or WooCommerce. To find out more about e-commerce platforms, see Section 8.3.

The good thing about blogging is that you can start small and add on as you go. So you might plan to start writing, then add your shop later on when you can afford it.

10.4 Content for your blog

The content on your blog is what will draw people to your site and is therefore pretty darn important. Without people coming to your site regularly, you won't be able to monetise it.

As discussed, if you want a successful blog, you need to develop a niche to help attract an audience. Whatever your focus is, you want to write engaging content that's fun and informative, as well as upload relevant photos or videos to keep your blog interesting.

The key to successful blogging is consistency and regularity. Don't just write a heap of blogs, publish them all at once, then not touch it again for months. Pick a time – say once a day or twice per week, whatever suits – and stick to it. The more consistent you are, the more Google likes you and you will rank higher; that is, your site will start to appear closer to the top of Google searches, meaning more people will find you.

Successful blog posts are generally about 600–850 words. They should have a clear focus and some engaging images (see Section 10.5 for more). Even if you think you have thousands of words to write on a subject, break up all that content into shorter posts of specific topics within your area of focus, as people like to read short pieces online. That way you'll have lots of content to keep readers engaged over a period of time.

A few tips when writing:
- Write how you speak – it gets your own voice across and sounds more natural.
- Make it very conversational, and ask questions at the end to be engaging.

- If you're citing something from another website, make sure you credit that website.
- Have a friend or partner proofread your work before it goes live.
- Offer value to your readers so they keep coming back.
- Keep a spreadsheet of all your blog ideas so that you have topics to write about when inspiration doesn't hit. Everyone gets writer's block now and again!

Even after you've put together a wonderful blog that attracts the attention of your readers and enjoys a steady increase in traffic every month, you have to bear in mind that for it to remain popular, you should constantly publish new material on the blog so as to keep it up to date. This will not be a problem if you have chosen a topic which you are familiar with.

A two-minute lesson on SEO

To help with search engine optimisation (also known as SEO, this relates to those Google rankings I mentioned), your posts should also contain the 'keyword' at least three times. The keyword is the main theme of the blog post. For example, if you were writing about online dating for mums, you'd make sure to use the phrase 'online dating for mums' at least three times within the blog post – making sure your post stays on theme without being too obvious or repetitive. 'Keyword stuffing' is where you use the keyword too much. For example: 'I'm using the keyword here to show you how the keywords work because I want the keywords to be the keywords in my blog so that my keywords make me rank higher in Google for my keywords.'

See what I did there? Don't do that. Google is pretty smart and can see what you're doing – and it won't help your ranking.

By doing a few specific things in each of your posts, you can improve how Google will rank your content compared to all other content on the same topic. If you rank well, your articles will appear towards the top of Google results – this means that an article is read frequently and is rich in content and more likely to answer the questions people are googling.

You can do a deep dive into SEO if you're interested, but here are some of the basics:

1. Include the keyword or phrase in the title of the article.
2. Include the keyword or phrase in the first paragraph of the article.
3. Write an inviting meta-description (the little bit of info that appears as a preview under each result in Google to tempt you to click through and read the article).
4. Link to another source article within the article.
5. Focus on only one keyword or phrase per article.
6. Ensure all your images are optimised by using alt-tags or alt-text; that is, a description of the image (using those keywords) for access-ibility purposes.

Hot tip: Write your blog in a Word document or Google Doc, then just copy and paste it over to your blog when you're done. The amount of work I have lost over the years because my blog has accidentally shut or I closed the window or the power went off makes me shudder.

Keep your blog posts consistent

It's a good idea to keep your posts quite consistent so readers know what to expect when they go to your blog. For example, each post might have a heading, an introduction, three paragraphs and then a conclusion. That said, it's always good to listen to feedback from your readers and adjust accordingly if they love one thing or don't like something else.

Your blog should also have a consistent tone, from the design to your writing voice to the images you use. This should reflect you and what you love – after all, that's why people are reading your blog! For example, I write a parenting blog, but I'm also into 1950s fashion. So my parenting blog has a real '50s feel that's reflected in all my images. Rock-abilly ladies, curlers, bowling shirts – you get the idea. It's my vision come to life on the internet. So infuse what you love into the blog, no matter your taste or style.

Where to get content if you aren't a writer

If you have a great idea for a blog but you're not much of a writer, you can hire people to write articles for you. Good writers will be able to match the tone of your blog, but you still need to oversee each article to make sure they meet your requirements. You want quality articles that provide relevant information, since it's one of the key points which attracts people to your blog. You can hire freelancer writers or use one of the many websites to find someone, such as:

- iWriter (a pay-per-article site)
- Hire Writers (a pay-per-article site; if you aren't happy with it, you reject it and another writer will do it)
- Content Development Pros (prices start at $12.95 per page)

10.5 Where to get images for your blog

You can't just go to Google and steal images for your blog – this is a breach of copyright. So you need to know where and how you are going to provide images for your blog. The best option is to take the photographs you need yourself. The best photos from blogs get shared on social media, including Pinterest and Instagram, which can help drive more readers to your blog. However, if you're not much of a photographer or don't have a good camera, there are loads of free or cheap photos available through stock photo sites (see pages 59–60, 181–183). This is especially handy if you need images that are impossible to take yourself.

Always check the terms and conditions before using and credit the photographer. When downloading images, make sure you size them correctly for the page so they look good when you preview your blog. Oh – always preview a blog post *before* you go live!

10.6 How to get traffic to your blog

Traffic refers to the volume of people who visit and read your blog. The more people who read your blog, the more advertising options open up to you and the more money you can make! When advertisers can see how popular your blog is with their target market, they realise that it's good value to promote their businesses on your blog.

You've already learned about generating great content for your readers, but how do you get them to come to your blog in the first place? Here are some ideas:

- Post links to your blog posts on social media and ask your friends and family to share them. Hopefully other people will check them out and share them with their own friends and family too.
- Do guest posts on other websites to encourage people to visit your blog or work with other bloggers to share each other's content.
- Make a 'Pinterest Pinnable' for every article you write. Pinterest is a great way to get traffic to your website.
- Make your blog 'infinite scroll' – that is, format it so that after someone reaches the end of an article, then the next article starts beneath it. This keeps eyeballs on your page for longer!
- Invite 'blog post suggestions' at the bottom of each page so readers can tell you what they want to read about next.

10.7 Monetise your blog

Okay – this is the big question. I know, I know, I keep talking about monetising your blog, but what does that actually mean? How does a blog make money? Well, the answer is in a lot of ways.

Once you've got some consistent traffic to your site, you can start looking at monetisation through a few different means. One of the simplest to is sell advertising space to other companies, usually in the form of ad banners that link through to the advertiser's own website. Another major source of income for bloggers is affiliate links (see

Chapter 11) and sponsored posts. Additional revenue streams you might add down the track if your blog is your core business include selling products or services (see Chapter 8), or you might be adding a blog to support an existing online shop and attract new buyers.

You're probably wondering how I monetised the Stay at Home Mum website. I use a combination of:

- Banner advertising
- Affiliate marketing
- Sponsored posts
- Product reviews
- Ebooks or digital downloads

Of course, not everyone who tries blogging is able to make a sustained income. However, perseverance and commitment will help increase your chances, especially if you have a kick-ass topic that people want to read about. The amount of work and effort you should put into your blog may be more than you had imagined at the beginning, especially when you're trying to kickstart it. Using a combination of methods is a good idea as most of them take a while to get established before you earn real money. Here is some more detail on these different revenue streams.

Banner advertising

Banner advertising is the ad blocks located at the top and down the sides on most websites these days. You can 'sell' the space on your website to specific companies who want to advertise to your readers or you can use a program such as Google AdSense that actually fills those spaces with available advertisements for you. Going through Google AdSense will generally earn you less money overall, but it does save a ton of time, as well as the trouble of finding suitable advertisers.

If people reading your blog click on an advertisement on your website, you get paid 'per click'. Some clicks are worth more than others. Most clicks are worth somewhere between 20c and $100 – it all depends on what niche you cover, what your customer is looking for and what the advertisement is. For example, a fashion outlet might get 5c per click, because fashion is popular and loads of people will click on it. Meanwhile, a brain surgeon advertisement – which is rarer – will get a much higher per-click rate, because it's a niche.

It's easy to set up a Google AdSense account, but you may have to get a developer to install the code for the advertisements (or closely follow the step-by-step instructions on YouTube). Once done, it's pretty much set-and-forget, and the money appears in your bank account every month – provided that some readers click on the advertisements.

Sponsored posts

A sponsored post is where an advertiser has paid you to write and post an article on your blog. It usually involves you mentioning a specific product or service and why you like it, and generally you agree as part of the deal to include photos and a link to buy the product or service. This is a longer form of the sponsored social media post, which we'll look at in Chapter 9. These articles could be about anything – think a new variety of yoghurt through to car insurance through to a fitness shoes – but always make sure that the product or service that you choose is a good fit for your audience. Blog readers expect to see sponsored posts but they'll think you're a sell-out if you are always posting random things that have nothing to do with your blog. If you can cleverly weave the product or service into you posts in a way that will appeal to your customers, you are selling the advertiser's wares and that's worth money to them.

Bloggers can charge anywhere from $5 to $10,000 for a sponsored article depending on their traffic. Expect to start on the lower end of this and work your way up as your blog becomes more popular.

Product reviews

Product reviews are where you are sent a product or given the chance to use a service, which you then provide assessment and feedback for. It's similar to doing sponsored posts but it's more about writing your honest feedback than selling the product – though, of course, the company who sent you the product hopes that you'll write a positive review to help generate sales for them. You're also less likely to get paid actual money for this, though if you have a substantial audience that the organisation really wants to reach, this becomes more likely.

Many newbie bloggers do product reviews in exchange for the product or service in the hope that that advertiser might pay for the privilege later on, but in all my years of blogging, I have never been paid by an advertiser who 'promises future payment for reviews'. It just doesn't happen. I'm not saying that you shouldn't take products in exchange for reviews only – that's up to you. It can be a good way to get content for your site and try new products, but unless you negotiate to get paid for your review, you're not going to earn cash.

Ebooks or digital downloads

Offering products for download on your blog are a fantastic way to earn some money – but of course you need the products and the functionality to sell things through your website. Check out Section 4.2 for my rundown about downloadable products you can sell.

Conclusion

I'm living proof that blogging can be a wonderful way to earn an income, and perhaps it will also provide an opportunity for you too? Hopefully this chapter has given you a solid intro to what's involved in starting a blog that you can monetise through advertising and sponsored posts. If you think this is for you, read on for another great revenue stream – affiliate marketing!

Chapter 11

Affiliate marketing

Affiliate marketing, which I mentioned briefly in the last chapter about monetising your blog, is something you can build into your website to generate what's called passive income; that is, having other people – the users of your site – make money for you. I like to think of affiliate marketing like a rolling stone gathering moss – the more you incorporate it into your business, the more money it will make. It does, however, take a bit of thought and time to get it up and running.

11.1 What is affiliate marketing?

Affiliate marketing involves promoting and selling other people's products or services on your own platforms – often a blog, but you can include affiliate links on other platforms, including your social media accounts. In its most basic form, you:

1. Choose a product that you love and fits your brand to promote/sell.
2. Join the seller's affiliate program and include the unique affiliate url in your own post.
3. Send traffic to that affiliate link using free and/or paid methods.
4. Get paid a commission if any of those visitors buy through your link.

You don't have to pick up the phone, speak to customers or get involved in the actual selling of the product (unless you want to, of course), as a well-designed website or system should do that for you.

There's a bit more strategy involved to really maximise the profit-making part of the process, but it's not that difficult to start making some money. And you don't need to have any special or technical skills to do it.

If you feel that affiliate marketing might be the right path for you, the first step is to educate yourself about what sells online, which demographic you will be selling to and where the best places are to post and promote links to ensure you start earning commissions.

11.2 The quickest and easiest way to get started

The quickest and easiest way to get started in affiliate marketing is to sign up to multiple affiliate platforms (I've drawn up a list for you further in the chapter). It is possible to set up your own affiliate contacts, but it's so much more work to find them and then do all the admin yourself. If you're just getting started, I would go with one of the established sites. Once you're signed up, grab the affiliate links and post the links with images of the product you're promoting on your website. Then you can use SEO and social media to push traffic through to your website. As the website traffic grows, so do the commissions earned through the website.

When you're just starting out, don't get discouraged if some advertisers or even affiliate companies knock back your application. Some of the larger advertisers are very finicky about who they work with. Just move on and promote the companies that want to work with you and keep building up your audience – sometimes it just takes time.

Once you're signed up, remember that the affiliate company is there to help you, so if you get stuck or are not sure what to do, ring, message or email them and get your issue sorted. I have no hesitation about telling large companies that their affiliate programs are hard to use, because if they want me to sell their product, I want it to be easy. You can do the same.

Hot tip: Never ever pay money to sign up to an affiliate marketing company!

11.3 Find products to link to

The best thing about affiliate marketing is that, unlike other kinds of online sales, you don't need to keep stock on hand, keep on top of orders or arrange postage. You can just find products or services you really love, that have relevance to your business or blog content, and start promoting them with a special link. The most effective affiliate marketing fits in with your usual content and actually enhances it – if your readers love your content, and your affiliate product links appeal to them too, they're far more likely to click through and buy, which is how you make money from it. This is a more organic way of approaching it rather than deciding on something to sell and then creating content around that. If you get it right, it won't seem like advertising and in fact your readers will love your recommendations. The key is to incorporate affiliate marketing as part of your blog from the start. This is how the successful bloggers use it to their advantage!

As well as thinking about what products you like that suit your content, you need to put some thought into what products or services your audience will actually buy. Who are your readers? Mostly women? People of all genders? What is their average level of income? Keep your eye on what is popular and talked about on your blog or Facebook page and what is trending in the broader industry.

The percentage of money you make through affiliate links is anywhere from 1–40% depending on the product. So linking to a $5 item may not be worth it unless you think your audience will buy a lot of them. At the other end of the spectrum, how many readers do you think will click through to buy an item over $500? You need to know your audience well, and it never hurts to do some trial and error with different types of products to see what your audience ends up buying. Then you can focus on items of that nature or at that price point.

11.4 How do you get paid?

When you sign up for an affiliate program, you will need to submit either your bank details or your PayPal account to get paid. The platform keeps track of the amount of clicks to the site, when sales are made and how much you make from each sale. You can run reports to see what products are selling, and which links are the most profitable. Payments are usually made when your affiliate balance reaches a milestone, such as $50.

How much money could I earn?

I get asked this all the time, but it's tricky to answer. Many affiliate marketers struggle to earn $100 a month, while I know some who earn five figures per day! It really does depend on a number of things, including your motivation, how much time you can put into it, the type of products you promote and how you go about promoting them. What I can share with you are a couple of tips to help you maximise your earning potential:

- Choose a product or service that provides a solution to a common but critical problem. Products and services that provide genuine relief will not only be helpful to others, but are usually more sought after than a nice-to-have product. They also tend to be in demand regardless of the economic climate.
- Promote 'high-ticket' digital products if you think your readership will be interested. High-ticket products are those that pay a commission of over $500 per sale. Digital products are things such as ebooks and online courses, which tend to pay well per sale because the production costs for merchants are usually one-off.

So, let's say you decide to promote something paying $500 per sale and your monthly income goal is $3000 per month. You would then need six online sales per month to earn what you need – are there at least six people reading your blog or visiting your site each month that you think would be interested enough and have the money to actually buy the item or service you're promoting?

How long does it take to make money?

Affiliate marketing is the sort of thing you need to spend time on regularly. By doing it consistently, you will build up an audience and then commissions. I've been doing affiliate marketing for about ten years now. It's a terrific source of income now – but it did take time.

The biggest gripe I hear is that people try affiliate marketing for a week or two, don't make any money and give up. If you want it to be a decent source of income, you need to spend a significant amount of time building links and checking your stats to ensure you are promoting the right products to the right demographic. Like any business, you need to spend time and energy on it to be successful. Can you dedicate a solid amount of time to work every single day?

Proper affiliate marketing is not a magic button that instantly generates income for you. Nothing is that easy. There are tools you can use to automate a lot of it, but you will still need to run the show. Whether you work eight hours a day or thirty minutes, it's important that you can work on your business every single day. I'm not saying it's always easy – what I'm saying is that it's simple. Learn the right way to do it, do it every day, and it can be a real way for you to earn a steady income.

11.5 So how do you actually do affiliate marketing?

Step 1: Apply to an affiliate platform

Sign up to one or all of the affiliate platforms listed in section 11.7. When you apply, you'll be asked for the link to your business and/or social media, website traffic details and bank account or PayPal details, plus how you intend to promote the advertiser. When you first start out, it's harder to be approved by advertisers, but if you take some time to answer all the questions with detailed, specific responses, you're more likely to be approved.

Step 2: Decide what you want to promote

Once you're approved to promote a business, the next step is to find the products or services that appeal to you, and that you think your followers will love or need. Choose only a few products to promote rather than a huge range, especially at first. You want to introduce them where relevant on your website, test the waters with your readership and most importantly, not seem too focused on the sales.

Step 3: Linking

The platform you're using should give you some instructions on how to link to the product you're promoting, but here is how most of them work. Once you've settled on a product, copy that product page's specific URL (because you want to link directly to a product, rather than just referring traffic to the home page of the company's website) and find the affiliate program's deep link section. Here, you paste in the URL and the platform will give you a new affiliate code, which you can copy and paste into your website in the relevant spot; that is, your post where you are recommending that your readers look at the product. And you're done!

Advertising

If you don't want to deep link a product or service, you can promote a business in its entirety by selecting a banner you can add to your website. Go to the advertising section and browse the ads to find one to suit your site.

> **Hot tip:** Always try to choose a banner that's close in colours and style to your website – this is known to increase the number of clicks, and therefore the number of sales.

Step 4: Affiliate links disclosure statements

It is best practice to disclose that you're using affiliate links, and this is required under law in some countries. Most advertisers have this as part of their sign-up process to help make sure you comply with this, so if you don't list your disclaimer and you get a sale, they can void it! The disclosure statement needs to be visible at the top of your website somewhere and be written in clear, simple language that's easy to understand. Here's a selections of statements – feel free to copy or adapt:

Disclosure: We use affiliate links to monetise our content. We may receive a commission on products or services that you purchase through clicking on links within this blog.

Disclosure: This is a review of a product or service. I am an independent blogger and the reviews are based on my own opinions; however, I may be compensated for sales made by the companies who produce the items.

Disclosure: This blog receives a commission for using affiliate links within our content. Although we receive commission for using and linking to these products, all of our opinions and suggestions are unbiased.

Disclosure: Any/all of the links on this website are affiliate links for which we receive a small commission from the sale of certain items, but the price remains the same for you.

Disclosure: I am an affiliate marketer with links to various online retailers on my website. When people read about products or services and then click on the links and purchase something, I earn a commission from the retailer.

11.6 How to engage an influencer to become an affiliate for your business

Now let's look at the affiliate marketing from the other side to see how affiliate marketing can serve *your* business as well as earn you income. If you have a product or service to sell, you can approach influencers with a relevant following to link to your site. Effectively, they do all the hard work of promoting your brand and selling your products, while you make more money and increase your brand exposure. Depending on what affiliate program you use, there is generally no cost to start up, and you pay a commission only on what the influencer or blogger actually sells. The harder the influencers work and market your products, the more you sell, and the more commission they receive. A good influencer has amazing traffic to their social media and will only promote products they love.

So how do you get the ball rolling? Well, just like when you are the one promoting the links, you sign up to a reputable affiliate marketing platform. Once signed up, you need to provide the platform with ways that influencers can promote your brand. This can include some or all of the following:

- Coupon codes
- Website banners of different sizes
- Discount codes
- Deep links
- Galleries
- Text links
- Videos
- Product images
- Data feeds

You can start simple and add more marketing material as you go along. If the influencer has a good following, you should start to see click throughs to your site when they post about your brand or product, and hopefully that will start turning into sales. You only pay the influencer (through the affiliate marketing platform) when this happens.

Hot tip: You have control as to which influencers promote your brand – or not. So if you know they won't be a good fit for you, you can decline them, just like the other way around!

11.7 Affiliate platforms and programs

The easiest way to start selling other people's products, or to find influencers to promote yours, is to join an affiliate platform. You only pay commission if an influencer directs customers to your business and you make a sale.

These are some established companies that run the affiliate side for a multitude of businesses. They will even give you tools to help you sell the products.

General affiliate programs

Commission Factory

This is an Australian affiliate platform. I love this platform – it's very user-friendly. The team is easy to work with, and if you have any problems, they're quick to respond to questions.

GrowthOps

This is an Australian growth marketing agency providing a range of services to businesses looking for growth – this includes an affiliate marketing component, operating on the Impact platform. It's been in the affiliate industry for a long time, previously as dgm and APD.

ShareASale

This is a US-based affiliate program that gives you a variety of options not found on other platforms, such as earning per click, average amount sale, average commission and reversal sale. ShareASale has been around for seventeen years, so it's stood the test of time, plus it's very easy to use compared to some other affiliate platforms. It also pays fast. The biggest niches on ShareASale include women's fashion, home and garden, green, business, family, insurance, legal and education; it's a plus for Australian audiences that many of their merchants are web-based services that don't incur huge shipping costs from the United States.

Amazon Affiliates or Amazon Associates

This is the biggest of the big. It's very easy to sign up, and you can promote just about any product that's featured on the Amazon website and get a cut. The downside with Amazon is that the commissions are generally very small.

ClixGalore

This is a great place for beginners to start. ClixGalore is worldwide, but has thousands of Australian companies listed to promote. It's less fussy with people who are novices joining their programs, and their links and banners are pretty easy to install. Most of the companies listed are up-and-coming small businesses trying to get their name out there.

Health and fitness affiliate programs

If you are a fitness blogger, health and wellness influencer or someone that has an online presence and want to support your following with some health and fitness recommendations – why not make some commission on the side? These are all Australian companies that offer an affiliate program that you can sign up with directly.

Fitness equipment affiliates

Gym and Fitness	Sportitude	Sam's Fitness
Trek Bikes	SMAI	Life Fitness
Workout Warehouse	CardioTech	Sportsmans Warehouse
Onsport	Mick Fanning Softboards	

Australian sports clothing affiliates

Sportitude	MassiveJoes	Proviz Sports
Insport	Doyoueven	Decathlon

Sportsmans Warehouse	Onsport	

Australian health and vitamin supplement affiliates

180 Nutrition	Aussie Health Products	Bulk Nutrients
Sportitude	Love Your Health	Love Thyself
MassiveJoes	True Protein	The Natural Nutritionist
Stoneage Health		

Sporting equipment affiliates

Sportsmans Warehouse	Onsport

Weight loss affiliates

WW (previously Weight Watchers)	CSIRO Total Wellbeing Diet	Shape Me
The Healthy Mummy	Great Ideas in Nutrition (Bariatric Surgery)	Fat Burners Only

Fashion affiliate programs
Fashion brands with affiliate programs

Ally Fashion	ASOS	Birdsnest
BNKR	Boohoo	Country Road
Crossroads	Cue	David Jones
Forever New	Glassons	Guess
The Iconic	JAG	Jo Mercer
Katies	Lorna Jane	Modcloth

R.M. Williams	Showpo	Supre
Tommy Hilfiger	Veronika Maine	UNIQLO
Atomic Cherry	Beginning Boutique	Beme
David Lawrence	Dotti	Freez
Frigirl	General Pants	Jacqui E
Jay Jays	Just Jeans	Nasty Gal Australia
Noni B	Peter Alexander	Portmans
Rockmans	W Lane	Cake Maternity
Autograph	City Chic	DayByDay

Small boutique and high-end fashion affiliates

Camilla and Marc	Ellery	Esther & Co
Fame & Partners	Forcast	Honey Peaches
Kabana Shop	Karen Millen Australia	Lane Crawford AU
Merino & Co	MinkPink	Missguided
Newchic	Pilgrim Clothing	SABA
Salty Crush	Stelly	YesStyle

Activewear and sports brands affiliates

Champion Australia	City Beach	New Balance
Nicky Kay	Rockwear	Salty Crush
Seafolly		

Low-cost imported clothing affiliates

AliExpress	DressLily	Fairyseason
Modlily	Rosegal	

Conclusion

There are so many benefits from making use of your blog to earn money through the web but it takes some thought, research and practice. Still feel like you could do with a bit of upskilling to give you your affiliate marketing edge? Surprisingly, it's hard to find decent and reputable online courses for affiliate marketing. Most affiliate platforms have a bit of a how-to guide; alternatively, Udemy offers a short online course.

Chapter 12

It's all about influence

Social influencing is a relatively new job where individuals earn a living by promoting brands, products and services to their online following. Some of the top global influencers net millions in revenue every year. Fun fact: nearly 20% of active YouTubers under the age of seventeen say that when they grow up, they want to be an influencer! So how on earth does it work?

To become an influencer, you need just that: influence. That means having a strong and loyal following on at least one of the many social media platforms, such as Instagram or YouTube. Your 'brand' (that is, you) is ideally about something specific that attracts an audience. For example, are you passionate about make-up? Do you love movies? Is the environment all you ever talk about? If you watch YouTube constantly and you love to talk about sports, then why not look at becoming a sports YouTuber? Just a note of caution: becoming a social media influencer may look like great fun from the outside, but it requires an incredible amount of work, dedication and hours.

In order to start charging for work, you need a number approaching 10,000 followers. Don't despair if you lack those kinds of numbers. Everyone has to start somewhere, so work on increasing those follower numbers. My biggest advice to aspiring influencers is to just be yourself because what makes you unique will be what ultimately attracts a loyal following. Keep doing what you're doing, do it well and try to have fun with it.

12.1 Types of influencers

An influencer is a person or brand that has a cult following. They have influence over the buying habits of the people who follow them. There are many types of influencers, and even subsets within those categories. But in broad terms, the main types of influencer are:

- YouTubers
- Instagrammers
- TikTokers
- Vloggers
- Brand ambassadors
- Bloggers
- Activists
- Journalists
- Photographers
- Reality TV stars
- Models
- Sports stars
- Actors and actresses

Subsets of influencer include:

- Gaming
- Sports
- Entertainment
- Beauty
- Comedy
- Sketches
- Education
- Music
- Film

Most of the largest influencers fit into these categories, but if you can think of a niche, however small, there'll be an influencer in that category!

A few years ago, the space was saturated with start-up influencers, which really affected the professionals. Many of these newbies have since fallen by the wayside (I think many don't realise just how hard the industry is) and the number has evened out. Many brands that employ influencers are also now more aware of how to analyse and choose potential influencers to ensure they get bang for their buck. You see, back in the 'old days' (which was only about five to seven years ago!) follower numbers could easily be fudged – and many people bought likes, which skewed the real number of passionate followers. Luckily those days are generally over, which is great for the real influencers with real followers. You only have to see some of the huge YouTube influencers now to know that influencer marketing is absolutely massive.

To give you an idea of how massive, here are some of the largest YouTubers in the world and their subscriber numbers at the time of print:

- Dude Perfect (sports influencer) – 54.8 million subscribers
- PewDiePie (gaming influencer) – 108 million subscribers
- Like Nastya Vlog (entertainment influencer) – 67 million subscribers
- T-Series (music influencer) – 169 million subscribers

Of course Americans dominate when it comes to major influencers, but we have a few biggies here in Australia too.

Hot tip: Social media is all about image. No, I'm not saying you need to be a supermodel to get work – you need to be yourself – but you do need amazing photographs for every social media platform. Invest in good-quality, individual photos that really show you being you. Employ a photographer with vision!

12.2 Influencer gigs

There are lots of different types of work you can get as an influencer, depending on what sort of influencer you are. Here's a rough guide:

- Product reviews
- Paid tutorials
- Sponsored articles
- Videos with product placement
- Affiliate marketing
- Advertising

Ensuring the work is a good fit

When applying for any influencer work, you need to ensure that the brand you intend to work with is a good fit for you. Ask yourself the following questions:

- Would you buy the product/service with your own money?
- Would you recommend the product or service to your friends or family?
- If no one was listening, would you still use it?

If all answers are yes, then the brand is a great fit. If not, you should either pass or not apply. Brands *hate* it when you waste their time, and they can sniff out a faker really quickly – as can your audience! See the discussion about choosing appropriate products for your audience in Chapter 11 about affiliate marketing. So don't waste their time and yours – only work with brands that are a good fit for you and your audience. As an influencer, you'll probably say no to more opportunities than you say yes to – but that's what makes your influence valuable. Authenticity is the key.

Applying for jobs

If your following is big enough, you'll have companies approaching you, but otherwise you'll need to get out there to find promotional work. If you already love a brand and you think your audience will love them too, approach the brand to see if they're interesting in paying you for your promotion. There are also a number of dedicated websites that advertise work for smaller influencers and bloggers – real paid work. Check out these sites.

Australia:
- The Right Fit – theright.fit
- Tribe Group – tribegroup.co
- Glass Door – glassdoor.com.au
- Pickstar – pickstar.com.au

United States:
- Scrunch – scrunch.com
- LinkedIn – au.linkedin.com/jobs
- Influence.co – influence.co
- Influencer – app.influencer.com/creator/signup
- Upfluence – upfluence.com
- AspireIQ – aspireiq.com/creators
- Post for Rent – postforrent.com/forinfluencers
- #Paid – hashtagpaid.com/creators
- HYPR – hyprbrands.com
- Open Influence – openinfluence.com
- Brand Backer – brandbacker.com/learn_blogs

A little instruction on how to go about applying for jobs as an influencer:

- Be positive and engaging. Read through the application carefully and make sure you fulfil all the criteria – just like applying for a normal job.
- Always ensure you include all of your social media handles and your contact details – the number of applications I've seen that don't include a phone number is baffling.
- Never start a message to a potential client with 'To whom it may concern'. This just shows you haven't done your homework. Do your research, find out more about the brand, and figure out who you'll be addressing and their position in the company. LinkedIn is a great place to research companies and position titles.

How much should you charge?

Sometimes you get to nominate your fee and sometimes companies will offer a set amount, and you can negotiate depending on the situation. Remember that the larger your following, the more money you can charge, especially if the company wanting you to promote them really wants to get their product in front of the audience you command! But my rule of thumb is to start small until you start getting some consistent work, then slowly increase your prices as you become more popular. To give you an example, my first sale was a 125x125 ad banner on my website promoting fairy clothing, for which I charged $15 per month. That's $15 extra per month, simply for some space on my website – and then once my following grew, I was able to charge more.

Try not to get into the habit of taking on any work for free – or else brands will expect it to always be free! PR agencies can be very persuasive – that's their job after all – and you may feel like the products or experiences they're offering in return are enough. But ultimately you want to earn money each time you promote a brand or product.

Conclusion

In this chapter, we had a good look at the rise of the influencer in today's online world. I hope it's inspired you to think about whether you could become one through the power of your brand and your following. Now we'll come back to earth so I can help you find some of the best tricks and tools for running your business efficiently and productively – there's nothing like a little help for the heavy lifting!

Chapter 13

Nifty tools for your new business

When you're starting up a new business or tapping into new ways to earn from home, it's only natural that you will be looking for a helping hand in the form of apps and software to make your life a little easier. Thankfully, there are many people who have acutely felt the pains of becoming self-employed, and they've invested plenty of time and money into creating solutions that we can now all enjoy.

13.1 Apps and websites for social media

Being able to schedule your social media posts ahead of time is great for small business owners as it means you don't have to be attached to your phone every moment of the day. Most of these apps and websites have free trials and free or low-cost start-up packages so you can test the waters before diving in.

Buffer	This allows you to schedule posts to Twitter, Facebook, Instagram, Instagram Stories, Pinterest, and LinkedIn, as well as analyse the results of the posts you send out into the world.

Later	This is great for Instagram because it has a visual content calendar. This allows you to schedule future posts easily and move around your planned posts with a drag-and-drop feature, so you can create the best-looking feed possible.
Sprout Social	This can help with Twitter, Facebook, Instagram, LinkedIn and Pinterest posting. It gives you a one-stop shop for analytics so you can see how each of them is performing.
Hootsuite	This can find and filter social conversations by keyword, hashtag and location – in multiple languages – to hear what people are saying about your brand, competitors and industry. It offers all the basics in its free version, but even more features if you choose to upgrade to one of the paid packages.
Tailwind	This specialises in Pinterest and Instagram scheduling.
Sendible	This can integrate with a huge number of platforms and is a great option for people who run social media for multiple businesses or clients, as you can create profiles for each to manage their respective campaigns.
SocialPilot	This is great for small business owners as you can post from your laptop, mobile or other device, plus it gives you content suggestions so you never run out of ideas.
TweetDeck	This was created in 2008 as an independent app, but is now officially part of the Twitterverse. For this reason, it's no surprise it specialises in managing content for Twitter accounts.
SocialOomph	This suits all social platforms and offers a stack of cool features, like 'self-destructing posts', which delete themselves after a set timeframe so your followers are not reading outdated content in the future.

13.2 Apps and websites for productivity and organisation

No matter whether you're a sole trader or working with a team, it's vital to keep track of what's happening within the business. Productivity apps are the ultimate non-judgemental accountability partner! Check out these options:

Trello	This is a web-based Kanban-style list-making app, to help you keep track of big-picture timelines and projects all the way down to the minutiae.
Basecamp	This is touted as the 'all-in-one tool for working remotely' and is great for teams.
Todoist	This app helps people organise their work and general life with to-do lists, task files, and ways to track productivity.
Asana	This is another great tool for remotely-connected teams. You can also use it as an individual to streamline your work, with to-do lists, boards, calendars, Gantt charts and more.
Slack	This is a business communication platform that allows you to connect with people through chat rooms that you can organise by topic. You can also direct message people in your network for fast and effective communication.
Sortd	This is designed to allow you to run your business communications with team members through your Gmail account.
Toggl	This is a time-tracking app that offers online time tracking and reporting services through its website, along with mobile and desktop applications.
HubSpot	This is more of a customer relationship management tool, but is also handy for you to organise your internal affairs.

13.3 Apps and websites for graphic design

If you don't know how to work with design products or any other photo-editing software out there, don't worry! You can learn how to use these programs through web tutorials and YouTube, but there are alternative ways to get the job done. Here are some graphic design websites for non-design people like you.

PicMonkey	This aims to give people an easy way to edit and design, providing a wide collection of templates for invitations, business cards, thank you cards, or just simple announcements. Its features are flexible and complete, making it perfect even for beginners! People all over the world are using it. It's free, but if you aren't satisfied with the features, you can upgrade to the Pro version for a fee.
Snappa	This is a favourite of many marketers and entrepreneurs because it's user-friendly and not too complicated for beginners. Its tools make graphic design easier and much quicker. All the templates and visual assets are professional, making it perfect for businesses, and you can get support if you encounter any problems.
Canva	This is probably my favourite photo-editing software available today. It's easy because it uses the drag-and-drop tool to create a design. If you want to work on the fly from your phone, you can download the application from the App Store or Google Play. Canva is free to use, but you do also have paid upgrade options.
Stencil	This lets you edit photos easily and quickly, and you can make logos and eye-catching designs with it, so it's perfect for social media and blogs.
DesignBold	This is a simple but powerful photo-editing tool that beginners won't find intimidating. Its aim is to empower everyone to realise their imagination, and is perfect for teams that want to design together.

Vectr	This is a software that's great for vector arts (which assures that images will always be crisp even if you resize), and offers easy-to-use tools that non-design people will love. If you can't figure out how to use some of its tools, you can browse through the website for simple tutorials and guides.
Lucidpress	This isn't only photo-editing software, it's also a publishing platform that has millions of users. It's an alternative to other design software for publishing, such as Adobe InDesign and Microsoft Publisher, with a wide range of templates, and is integrated with Google Drive and Google Apps.
Crello	This photo-editing software is great for social media, emails, ad banners, blogs and posters. You can find millions of photos, thousands of templates, and over 30 design formats. If you want to learn about graphic design, you can also find tips on their website. It's free to use, or you can pay to upgrade to the Pro version.
Easil	Easil is easy to use with thousands of professional-looking, customisable templates, and lots of stock images. You can also save colour palettes, make animations and add shadows to text. The customer service is great, and you can even get design assistance. You can use it for free, but if you want access to all its features, you can upgrade to 'Plus' or 'Edge' versions.

13.4 Apps and websites for your finances

Managing the moolah as it comes in and flows out is important for any business owner. Not all of us are numbers people, so it's great to have some tools to keep you kicking goals. Here's my round-up.

PayPal	This has become synonymous with e-commerce, and remains one of the most recognised ways to send and receive funds online. Although you will be charged a small fee for every transaction for the privilege of using the service, you know that you have the backing of this global brand and a team who are always helpful when it comes to investigating any weird things going on with your account.
Stripe	This is nipping at the heels of PayPal as a widely recognised way to take payments for your business. Its fees differ from PayPal's, so I advise that you check out both and see which will work best for you, especially if your business involves a lot of international transactions.
Afterpay	This allows customers to buy from you now, but split up their payments into four interest-free instalments. Meanwhile, you still get paid upfront! There are fees involved to offer this, but if you're selling high-ticket items, or have customers who are likely to buy several moderately-priced items in one go, this can be an attractive way for them to buy from you.
Zip Pay	This is another 'buy now, pay later' system. It takes all the risk of each transaction, guaranteeing that once an order is made, you will receive payment. However, unlike Afterpay the money will only come into your account as the customer pays, so your income from a sale will be spread out over the timeframe you nominate for your customers.
Google Pay	This is a digital wallet platform and online payment system developed by Google for mobile devices, enabling users to make payments with Android phones, tablets or watches.
Apple Pay	This lets you make secure purchases in stores, in apps, and on the web – and now send and receive money from friends and family right there in Messages.

And some great accounting software for small businesses.

QuickBooks	This is great for smaller businesses. You can self-manage your budget and use it to accept business payments, manage and pay bills, and for payroll functions if you have a team.
FreshBooks	This is cloud based so you can use it on your phone or laptop. It has automated invoicing options and links directly to your bank accounts, so payments are received and reconciled faster.
Microsoft Office Accounting	This is excellent if you're using the Office suite for other elements of your business, as it's fully integrated with this. You can do all of your accounting, see bank feeds and operate a payroll through this option.
Sliptree	This offers free templates so that you can create simple invoices that look great on screen and paper.
Xero	This is basically like having an accountant living in your computer! It has a comprehensive suite of services, and there are plenty of how-to videos on YouTube to help beginners get started with setting it up. Xero can produce profit-and-loss and cashflow statements at the click of a button; your accountant can use your Xero accounts to easily process your tax returns and manage your GST and tax commitments – one less thing for you to worry about!

Conclusion

In this chapter, I introduced to you to some of the technology that can make your life easier when running your own business, from accounting software to productivity apps. With a little help from these clever tools and programs, you don't need to be a design whiz or stay glued to your phone all day – you can get on with doing the interesting stuff you do best!

The next chapter is the very last, and a really important one – how to survive your first huge year earning money from home, in whatever form that takes.

Chapter 14

Surviving the first year

I'm not going to sugar-coat it – being in business is hard. The first year is usually the hardest, but it can also be the best.

For the first year, you're still learning about processes, how to deal with customers, complaints, lack of funds (there are never enough funds in the first year) and, most significantly, failures.

Failures can make you feel like you just want to throw the computer through a wall and go to bed. But I can assure you that those failures of your first year will teach you more about business than everything you learn in the subsequent years. So, try to see them as challenges and opportunities to learn and grow, rather than failures. Reframing and moving forward will help you achieve your goals far more than beating yourself up for making a mistake.

Let me show you a little of what I learned my first year of running Stay at Home Mum through the challenges I faced.

Accounting

We all know accounts are an imperative part of any business, but if you've never had to balance accounts before, this can be a huge challenge. I encourage you to get a good accountant or bookkeeper who can steer you in the right direction.

A professional can also help you prepare BAS (business activity statements), other taxes, help with GST and, if you are lucky enough to be able to employ another person, with payroll, superannuation and WorkCover.

Accounts are an area you really can't muck around with – so my tip is to reserve your energies for what you're confident with and get help from the experts for everything else.

Work processes

If you make a product as part of your business, the processes involved, from getting that product manufactured through to the actual selling of it can take a while to get right. And that's what can get you the odd bad review out there on social media, especially if there are delays in delivery. So when it comes to your processes, put your customers first and write a checklist to ensure every single item from manufacturer to packaging and postage is produced and handled in exactly the same high-quality manner. Over time you'll be able to streamline these processes so they're as efficient as possible.

Write down these processes as you establish them, and keep them updated, so that if and when you put staff on, you already have a manual for how to do things.

Social media platforms

Just when you think you're busy enough, now you have to find time for marketing and publicity, including producing content on social media platforms, keeping them updated, and answering any questions, enquiries or complaints that come through these platforms.

This can do your head in if you're not careful! As important as social media is, it can be full of time-wasters and tyre-kickers. To keep on top of all this, create a list of frequently asked questions (FAQs) for your website, if you have one, and set up template responses for answering questions through social media and email. Between these two strategies, you can pre-empt a lot of enquiries and save hours every day.

Keep on keeping on

Finally, and this is a big one, it's common in the first year to just want to give up. This is where your passion and persistence need to kick in. Many new businesses don't make a dollar of profit in the first year – can you weather that storm? Can you stand seeing a bad review on social media or receiving an email of complaint? It's going to be difficult at times. And it's okay to fall apart. As long as when you do that, you get straight back up and keep going.

Conclusion

The first year of any new endeavour is often the toughest – you'll have that learning curve, those unexpected obstacles, and any number of setbacks and discouragements. It may take time to see the glimmers of success come through. That's completely normal for a new business – ask anyone who's done it.

Hang in there, ask for help wherever you can, and outsource whatever you can – whatever it takes to get through to sunnier pastures!

Final word

Like anything worthwhile in life, it takes work and time to make money in your own business, whether that be online or offline, a fully-fledged business or some income on the side. Many say that it seems as if starting a business is a bit like climbing a mountain – it's just too hard. Well, my answer to that is, 'If it was easy, wouldn't everyone be doing it?'

I love waking up every day and actually being excited to get to work. Not every day is easy, and some weeks positively suck, but I wouldn't ever want to be doing anything else. I'm the master of my own destiny. If I want more money, I work a bit harder. When I need a break, I can back off a bit and take time out with my family. That's why I think starting your own business, whether casual or full time, is perfect for mums!

In all seriousness, I'm not the sharpest crayon in the box, but I'm tenacious and hardworking. And if I can run my own successful business and provide for my family under my own steam, then I say you have a damn good chance of doing it too.

So dream big, and start a spreadsheet on how you can realise your amazing idea. And if you want to make a go of it, you will.

I wish you all the best!

Appendix

Still thinking about the best idea for casual earning or fully-fledged business? Scan through these tables for inspiration. Some have been discussed in detail already, but there might just be something in here that you hadn't thought about before . . . As always, do you research before starting any new endeavour, make sure you know about any legal requirements, insurance or certification you might need, and most of all, have fun earning!

Food business ideas

Food delivery service	Salad vending machine	Healthy snack subscription boxes
Bottled marinades and sauces	Food truck	Keto menu planner
Gourmet popcorn	Gourmet confectionery	Herb grower
Ice cream shop	Meal planner	Micro brewery
Sell homegrown vegetables at a local market	Nutrition consultant	Online cooking classes
Party food catering	Flavoured vinegars	Salads to go

Coffee delivery service	Sell homemade gourmet muesli or granola	Sell your own honey
Personal cook	Make and sell hot breakfasts at local markets	Coffee bean subscription boxes
Start your own cooking YouTube channel	Fresh pasta	Food allergy personal shopper
Gourmet sandwiches	Snack subscription boxes	Food blogging
Start a community garden	Gluten-free food shop	Cake-decorating equipment supplier
Personalised candy	Barbecue catering	Pet food and treats
Online organic food supermarket	Gourmet doughnuts	Sell spice blends, such as barbecue seasoning
School lunch preparation service	Bespoke tea salon	Mobile pizza oven
Frozen yogurt shop	Bespoke food platters	Organic food boxes
Wine tasting evenings	Wine subscriptions	Wedding desserts
Weekly fruit and vegetable box delivery service	Romantic dinner planner	Cheesecakes
Vegan chocolate supplier	Raw desserts	Raw bliss balls
High tea service	At-home smoking kits	Gourmet food and wine hampers
Pre-made vegetarian meal supplier	Sell dehydrated fruits and vegetables	Bespoke cake mixes
Frozen gourmet pizzas	Flavoured marinated feta cheese	

Most business ventures in the health industry will require accreditation. But there are a few you can do without acquiring a university degree, although they will require some upskilling.

Herbalist	Massage therapist	Health blogger
Health podcaster	Wellness coach	Crime scene clean-up
Weight loss coach	Medical transcriptionist	Doula
Respite care	Home healthcare	Aged care equipment rental
Sell health supplements	Put together first aid boxes	Sell medical textbooks
Fitness equipment rentals	Personal trainer	Sports equipment rental
Design activewear	Vegan cooking	Keto cookbook

Business ideas with animals

Pet sitting	Aquarium maintenance	Pet photographer
Dog obedience training	Dog walking service	Bespoke pet treats
Homemade dog food delivery service	Doggie daycare	Pet subscription boxes
Dog washing service	Sell pet beds	Bespoke pet clothing
Pet taxi service	Rent a goat service	Goat yoga
Pet proofing service	Invisible pet fencing	Sell tropical fish
Chicken supplies	Sell aviaries	Bee hotels
Online pet supplies	Make pet memorial jewellery	Pet cremation service
Cute animal calendar	Petting zoo	Wildlife photographer

Make and sell horse rugs	Pet transportation service	Supply ponies for a 'unicorn' birthday party
Horse riding		

Business ideas in the education sector

Sell online lessons plans	Create an online learning website	Make educational toys
Home schooling website	Online book shop	Start a book club
Start a local newsletter	Make and sell ebooks	Start an educational YouTube channel
Adult learning centre	Write a children's book	Teach a musical instrument
Ghost writing	Career counsellor	Family history researcher
Grant writing	School fundraising consultant	Translator service
Home daycare		

Businesses you can start online

Blogger or influencer	Design logos	Website designer
Graphic artist	Graphic designer	Local marketing consultant
Write resumes	Instagram marketing	Start a podcast
Buy and sell on Ebay	Dropshipping	Sell stock photography
Ebook writer	Virtual assistant	Copywriting
Website testing	Print on demand business	Teach online courses

Business coach	Online tutor	Travel consultant
Online researcher	Public relations consultant	Online newsletter writer
Erotic story writing	Sell sex toys	Online dating consultant
Event planner		

Business ideas in the arts, crafts and entertainment industry

Design a business diary	Arts and crafts subscription boxes	Teach animation online
Create and sell your own line of chalk paint	Paint people's pet portraits	Design tattoos
Make handmade wedding invitations	Bespoke jewellery	Sell a piece of your own music to a music stock site
Interior decorator	Personal stylist	T-shirt slogan designer
Kids face painter	Dance teacher	Voice-over artist
Make candles	Make soaps	Children's party entertainment
Make gift baskets	Online art lessons	Scrapbooking supplies
Clothing alterations	Fashion designer	

Business ideas that focus on the home and car

Pool cleaner	House cleaner	Window cleaner
Housekeeper	House sitter	Professional organiser
Meal preparation	Ironing service	Laundry service
Nappy service	Lawn-mowing service	Gardening service
Home cook	Car detailing	Packing services
Home staging service		

Seasonal business ideas

Christmas tree decorator	Christmas cooking	Gift wrapping service
Personal shopper	Make and sell christmas wreaths	Lawn mowing and garden maintenance
Pool cleaner	Bike rental service	

Low-cost business ideas

Start a blog	Write an ebook	Write erotic fiction
Drive for Uber	Freelance writing	Car washing and detailing
Resume service	Digital product sales	Stock photo sales
Pet sitting	Recycling service	

Business ideas you can start today

Do gigs on Fiverr	Airtasker	Uber driver

Acknowledgements

Thank you to my wonderful husband for his unwavering support. To my business partner, Nicole, whom I love like a sister, and to the people of Gympie, my hometown, for always believing in me.

Discover a
new favourite

Visit **penguin.com.au/readmore**